Filesystem Management and Backup Strategies for SysAdmins

James Relington

DEDICATION

To those who seek knowledge, inspiration, and new perspectives—
may this book be a companion on your journey, a spark for curiosity,
and a reminder that every page turned is a step toward discovery.

AKNOWLEDGEMENTS

I would like to express my deepest gratitude to everyone who contributed to the creation of this book. To my colleagues and mentors, your insights and expertise have been invaluable. A special thank you to my family and friends for their unwavering support and encouragement throughout this journey.

Introduction to Filesystem Management

Filesystem management is a fundamental aspect of system administration that directly impacts the efficiency, security, and scalability of an organization's infrastructure. At its core, filesystem management involves the configuration, maintenance, and optimization of the storage systems within an operating system. It includes tasks like organizing and maintaining files, managing disk space, ensuring data integrity, and implementing backup solutions. As data volumes grow and storage technologies evolve, the ability to effectively manage filesystems becomes increasingly complex, demanding a comprehensive understanding of various filesystem types, tools, and best practices. This chapter provides an introduction to filesystem management, offering insights into its importance and core concepts for system administrators.

A filesystem is a method used by an operating system to store, organize, and retrieve files from a storage device. It dictates how files are named, stored, accessed, and organized on disk drives. Filesystems provide an interface between the operating system and physical storage devices, which can include hard drives, solid-state drives, and networked storage systems. Different types of filesystems offer various features that cater to specific use cases, such as performance optimization, data redundancy, or compatibility with certain operating systems. The system administrator must decide which filesystem is appropriate based on these needs and configure it to work efficiently with the underlying hardware.

Understanding filesystem structure is crucial in the management process. A typical filesystem consists of directories and files that are organized in a hierarchical structure, much like a tree. The root directory serves as the starting point for this structure, with directories branching out to accommodate various subdirectories and files. Each file within the system has specific attributes, including its name, size, permissions, and location within the filesystem. The filesystem also relies on metadata to track these files and directories. This metadata is stored in data structures known as inodes, which contain information about the file's properties, such as ownership, timestamps, and access control information. Managing these inodes efficiently is essential for maintaining the integrity and performance of the filesystem.

Filesystems also play a significant role in ensuring data integrity and reliability. One of the critical challenges faced by system administrators is the potential for filesystem corruption, which can result from hardware failures, software bugs, or improper shutdowns. In some filesystems, journaling is employed to provide a safeguard against corruption. Journaling filesystems keep a log of changes that are to be made, allowing the system to recover to a consistent state in the event of a failure. Non-journaling filesystems, on the other hand, do not maintain this log and may require more extensive checks and repairs if an issue occurs. Understanding the underlying mechanics of filesystem consistency is vital for administrators to prevent data loss and system downtime.

Filesystem performance is another critical factor that system administrators must manage. The efficiency of a filesystem affects how quickly data can be read from and written to the storage device, which in turn impacts the overall performance of the system. Factors such as disk fragmentation, disk caching, and file access patterns can influence filesystem performance. For example, in environments with large numbers of small files, the performance of the filesystem might degrade unless it is optimized for such workloads. Filesystem tuning, which involves adjusting settings like block sizes, file caching mechanisms, and read/write strategies, can help improve performance for specific use cases.

Another important aspect of filesystem management is disk space utilization. As files are created, modified, and deleted, the storage space on a disk becomes fragmented, and unused space may not be readily reclaimed. Proper disk space management involves monitoring storage usage, identifying areas of inefficiency, and ensuring that disk space is not wasted. Filesystem tools allow administrators to check disk usage, identify large or obsolete files, and optimize storage allocation. Disk quotas can also be implemented to limit the amount of disk space individual users or groups can consume, preventing one user from consuming all available resources.

Effective filesystem management is also closely tied to backup and recovery strategies. A robust backup system ensures that, in the event of data loss or system failure, critical files can be restored quickly and with minimal disruption. Administrators must carefully plan backup schedules, retention policies, and storage locations. A comprehensive backup strategy might involve full backups, incremental backups, or differential backups, depending on the needs of the organization. Additionally, the system administrator must consider the physical and virtual environments where the filesystem resides. For instance, managing a filesystem in a cloud-based environment may require different tools and strategies compared to managing a local or on-premises system.

In modern computing environments, virtualization and cloud storage have added new layers of complexity to filesystem management. Virtualized environments often use virtual disks that are stored on physical disks managed by hypervisors. These virtual disks can be managed through specialized tools that allow administrators to allocate storage to virtual machines dynamically. Cloud-based filesystems, such as those provided by Amazon Web Services, Google Cloud, and Microsoft Azure, offer scalability and redundancy but require a different approach to management, including considerations for network latency, data transfer costs, and security.

As the volume of data grows, the need for advanced filesystem management tools has become more pronounced. Tools such as disk partitioning software, file recovery utilities, and system monitoring tools allow administrators to streamline their workflows and ensure that filesystems are properly managed. These tools provide vital insights into disk health, filesystem performance, and storage utilization, making it easier to detect and resolve issues before they become critical problems.

In summary, filesystem management is a critical component of system administration that requires an in-depth understanding of various filesystems, their structure, performance characteristics, and security considerations. System administrators must be able to choose the right filesystem for their needs, configure it effectively, and ensure its ongoing maintenance and optimization. By mastering the intricacies of filesystem management, administrators can maintain high levels of system performance, reliability, and data integrity. This foundational knowledge not only supports the efficient operation of individual systems but also contributes to the overall success of an organization's IT infrastructure.

Filesystem Types and Their Uses

Filesystem types represent the fundamental frameworks through which operating systems interact with storage devices. Each filesystem is designed with specific goals in mind, from optimizing performance to ensuring data security or enabling compatibility across diverse systems. As system administrators, understanding the characteristics, benefits, and limitations of each filesystem type is crucial for selecting the most appropriate solution for different use cases. The choice of filesystem affects the overall efficiency, scalability, and reliability of the system, making it one of the key decisions in filesystem management. In this chapter, we will explore various filesystem types, how they operate, and where they are typically used.

One of the most widely used filesystem types is the Extended File System, or ext, primarily found in Linux-based operating systems. Developed as an improvement over the original Minix filesystem, ext has undergone several revisions to meet the growing demands of modern systems. The most recent iteration, ext4, is known for its excellent performance, robustness, and support for large files. Ext4 offers advanced features like journaling, which logs file changes to protect against data corruption in case of a system crash or power failure. This filesystem type is commonly used in Linux servers, desktops, and embedded systems. Its flexibility and reliability make it an excellent choice for general-purpose use, particularly where stability and compatibility are important.

Another important filesystem type is the NTFS, which stands for New Technology File System. Developed by Microsoft for its Windows operating systems, NTFS is designed to offer high-performance storage with advanced features like file encryption, access control, and disk quotas. NTFS supports large volumes and files, making it suitable for modern hard drives with high storage capacities. Its ability to manage both metadata and user data efficiently allows it to perform well in environments that require complex file structures. NTFS is often used in business environments, personal computers, and servers running Windows, particularly when there is a need for robust data protection and security features. While NTFS works best within Windows, it can be accessed by other operating systems, though with some limitations regarding compatibility.

FAT, or File Allocation Table, is an older filesystem type that has evolved over time. Initially designed for use in floppy disks and early hard drives, FAT is still used in systems that require simplicity and broad compatibility. FAT32, a common variant, is supported by virtually every operating system, including Windows, Linux, and macOS. Despite its age, FAT32 remains useful for external storage devices like USB flash drives, memory cards, and other portable media. Its simplicity is both an advantage and a limitation. While FAT32's straightforward design ensures fast access and ease of use, it lacks features like file permissions and journaling, making it unsuitable for complex or high-security environments. Nevertheless, its cross-platform compatibility makes it an ideal choice for transferring files between different operating systems.

The HFS+ (Hierarchical File System Plus) is the default filesystem used by macOS, Apple's operating system for desktop and laptop computers. It provides a rich set of features, including file system journaling, support for file and folder permissions, and the ability to handle large volumes and files. HFS+ has been optimized for performance on Mac hardware, taking full advantage of Apple's hardware capabilities. One of the distinguishing features of HFS+ is its ability to support metadata, which allows for rich file attributes like custom icons, file attributes, and even file search indexes. However, Apple has transitioned to a newer filesystem, APFS (Apple File System), for its most recent macOS versions. While APFS is set to become the future of file management on macOS, HFS+ remains prevalent in older Mac devices and certain legacy applications.

The ZFS (Zettabyte File System) is another advanced filesystem, initially developed by Sun Microsystems and now widely used in enterprise environments. ZFS stands out for its exceptional scalability and data integrity features, including built-in checksums that verify the integrity of data and automatically repair corrupted files. ZFS also supports snapshots, allowing system administrators to create backups of the filesystem at a particular point in time without shutting down the system. This capability is particularly useful for data-heavy environments like databases and virtualization platforms. ZFS can also handle large amounts of data without compromising performance, making it well-suited for high-volume servers and storage arrays. While ZFS offers powerful features, it is most commonly used on systems running Solaris, FreeBSD, or Linux with additional tools, and is not natively supported by Windows or macOS.

ReFS (Resilient File System) is a modern filesystem developed by Microsoft, designed to address some of the limitations of NTFS, particularly in terms of data integrity and error correction. ReFS is optimized for high reliability and is built to handle large volumes of data while providing features like integrity streams, which protect data from corruption. It is particularly well-suited for environments that require continuous availability and minimal downtime, such as data centers and large-scale file storage systems. However, ReFS does not support all the features of NTFS, such as booting and file compression, making it unsuitable for general-purpose desktop use. ReFS is more commonly used in specialized applications like storage pools and virtual machine environments in Windows Server.

The Btrfs (B-tree File System) is a modern filesystem for Linux that emphasizes scalability, data integrity, and advanced features such as snapshotting, compression, and self-healing. Btrfs is designed to overcome some of the limitations of traditional filesystems like ext4, offering features that are particularly useful for managing large amounts of data in cloud environments and enterprise systems. Like ZFS, Btrfs supports snapshots, which allows administrators to create consistent backups of the filesystem. This feature makes it especially useful in situations where data protection and disaster recovery are critical. However, Btrfs is still considered experimental in some areas and may not be as stable as more mature filesystems, though it is actively developed and increasingly adopted for production systems.

Each filesystem type serves different purposes and has its advantages and disadvantages. For system administrators, selecting the appropriate filesystem type depends on several factors, including the operating system being used, the performance requirements, and the need for features such as data integrity, scalability, or security. By understanding the various filesystem types and their specific use cases, administrators can make informed decisions that best support the goals of the organization and ensure the optimal performance and reliability of the system.

Understanding Filesystem Hierarchy

Filesystem hierarchy is the structured arrangement in which files and directories are organized on a storage device. It provides a logical way to manage and access data, ensuring that files are stored efficiently and are easy to locate. Understanding the filesystem hierarchy is crucial for system administrators, as it helps in managing files, controlling access, and ensuring the smooth functioning of the system. The hierarchy forms the foundation of any operating system's file management system, and a solid grasp of its structure is essential for configuring, maintaining, and troubleshooting systems effectively.

At the heart of the filesystem hierarchy is the concept of directories and subdirectories. A directory serves as a container for files and other directories, and subdirectories are simply directories within directories. This tree-like structure starts at a single root, which acts as the top-level directory. Every file and directory in the system can be traced back to this root directory, making it the central point of reference. The root directory is often represented by a single forward slash (/) in Unix-based systems, and its existence is crucial for the system to function. All other directories and files are structured beneath the root, creating a path that leads from the root to any specific file or directory.

In Unix-like operating systems, including Linux, the filesystem hierarchy is standardized by the Filesystem Hierarchy Standard (FHS), which defines where files and directories should be located to maintain consistency across systems. This standardization allows administrators and users to navigate filesystems with a clear understanding of where specific types of files are stored. For example, system binaries are typically located in the /bin directory, essential libraries in /lib, and configuration files in /etc. This consistent structure helps ensure that system management tasks such as backups, software installation, and troubleshooting are performed efficiently.

One of the key elements of the filesystem hierarchy is the separation of system files from user files. This distinction helps in organizing the data more effectively and ensures that system integrity is maintained. System files, which are required for the operating system to function, are generally stored in directories like /bin, /sbin, and /lib. These files include executable programs, system libraries, and other essential components that are needed for the operating system to run. User files, on the other hand, are stored in directories such as /home or /usr. The /home directory contains individual user directories, where each user's personal files and settings are stored. The /usr directory is used for user programs, libraries, and documentation that are not essential for the system's boot process but are still critical for day-to-day operations.

Within the hierarchy, directories such as /var and /tmp serve specific purposes as well. The /var directory holds variable files, including logs, databases, and other data that can change in size or content during normal system operation. This directory is important for managing dynamic data that must be kept track of over time, such as log files that record system events or error messages. The /tmp directory, on the other hand, is used for temporary storage of files that are created and discarded by applications or the operating system during operation. Files in /tmp are often deleted automatically after a certain period or once the system is restarted.

Another important directory in the filesystem hierarchy is /dev, which contains device files. These files are special files that represent hardware devices such as hard drives, network interfaces, and peripherals. Rather than accessing hardware directly, users and programs interact with device files, which abstract the complexities of interacting with hardware directly. The /dev directory is essential for enabling communication between the operating system and the underlying hardware.

In addition to the standard directories defined by the FHS, modern operating systems may include other directories for specific use cases. For example, in multi-user environments, it is common to see directories like /srv, which is used for data specific to services provided by the system, or /opt, where optional software packages are installed. These directories help maintain the organization of files and ensure that data associated with specific services or software is stored in an appropriate location.

One of the most important aspects of filesystem hierarchy is the concept of permissions and ownership. Each file and directory within the hierarchy has an associated owner and permissions that dictate who can access or modify the file. These permissions are integral to maintaining system security and ensuring that users can only interact with files in ways that are appropriate to their roles and responsibilities. For example, a system administrator may have the ability to modify system files stored in directories like /etc or /usr, while regular users may only have access to their own files in the /home directory. Understanding the filesystem hierarchy, along with how permissions and ownership work, is crucial for maintaining a secure and well-organized system.

As data storage requirements grow, filesystem hierarchy also helps to manage the allocation of space on physical storage devices. Filesystems organize data into blocks, and each file is stored in one or more blocks on the storage medium. The hierarchical structure makes it easier for the operating system to locate and retrieve these blocks, ensuring that data can be accessed quickly and efficiently. By managing how space is allocated and how data is indexed, the filesystem hierarchy plays a vital role in optimizing storage utilization and minimizing fragmentation.

In modern computing, understanding the filesystem hierarchy is more critical than ever, especially with the increasing complexity of storage systems. Virtualized environments, cloud storage, and distributed systems all rely on a clear, structured approach to data management. Even though the underlying principles of filesystem hierarchy remain the same, the way it is applied can vary significantly in these environments. For example, cloud storage may involve virtual filesystems that abstract the physical location of data, while distributed filesystems require careful management of data replication and consistency across multiple nodes.

System administrators must be well-versed in the filesystem hierarchy to perform routine maintenance tasks like installing software, managing system updates, and backing up data. Furthermore, understanding the structure of the filesystem can aid in troubleshooting issues such as file corruption or missing data. By knowing where certain types of files are stored, administrators can quickly identify problems and resolve them more effectively.

The filesystem hierarchy provides the foundation for the entire file management system of an operating system. It offers an organized way to store and access files, ensuring that both system files and user data are stored in a manner that supports both performance and security. The structured approach to organizing data within directories not only improves system efficiency but also allows for easier management, maintenance, and troubleshooting. By adhering to standardized directory structures and understanding how data is stored, system administrators can maintain a well-functioning system that meets both the operational needs and security requirements of the organization.

File Permissions and Ownership

File permissions and ownership are fundamental concepts in filesystem management, especially in multi-user operating systems like Linux and Unix. They define who can access and modify files, thus playing a crucial role in system security and data integrity. The proper management of file permissions and ownership ensures that sensitive files are protected from unauthorized access while allowing legitimate users the necessary access to perform their tasks. In environments where multiple users and processes interact with a shared filesystem, the ability to control who can read, write, or execute files is essential for maintaining order and preventing malicious or accidental misuse of system resources. Understanding how file permissions and ownership work allows system administrators to effectively manage and secure their systems.

At the core of file permissions is the concept of access control. File permissions dictate the level of access a user has to a particular file or directory. These permissions are typically assigned to three distinct user categories: the file owner, the group associated with the file, and all other users on the system, often referred to as "others." The owner of a file is typically the user who created the file or the user who has been explicitly assigned ownership. The group is a set of users that share a common interest or responsibility, and the permissions granted to the group apply to all members of that group. Lastly, the "others" category includes all users who are not the file owner and do not belong to the file's group. This three-tier system provides flexibility, allowing for granular control over who can access or modify files.

The permissions themselves fall into three main types: read, write, and execute. Read permission allows a user to view the contents of a file, but not to modify it. Write permission, on the other hand, grants the ability to modify the file, which includes adding, deleting, or altering its content. Execute permission is used for files that are executable, such as scripts or programs, allowing the user to run the file as a command. These permissions are not only applied to individual files but can also be assigned to directories. For directories, read permission allows a user to list the files contained within, write permission allows a user to create, delete, or rename files within the directory, and execute permission enables a user to enter the directory and access its files.

Permissions are typically represented using a symbolic notation or numeric notation. In symbolic notation, permissions are represented by a series of characters, such as "rwxr-xr--," where each character corresponds to a specific permission for the owner, group, and others. The first character represents the file type, such as a dash (-) for a regular file or a "d" for a directory. The next three characters represent the owner's permissions, the following three characters represent the group's permissions, and the final three characters represent the permissions for others. In numeric notation, permissions are represented as a three-digit number, where each digit corresponds to the permissions for the owner, group, and others. The digits are calculated by assigning numerical values to the read (4), write (2), and execute (1) permissions. For example, a permission set of "rwxr-xr--" translates to the numeric value 755, indicating full permissions for the owner, read and execute permissions for the group, and read-only permissions for others.

File ownership, like permissions, is an essential part of controlling access to files. Each file and directory is associated with an owner and a group. The owner is typically the user who created the file, but ownership can be transferred to other users using commands like chown. The group, in contrast, is a collection of users who share common permissions to access the file. Groups are particularly useful in multi-user systems where users need to collaborate and share access to certain files while maintaining restricted access to others. For instance, a group may be created for a specific project, and files related to that project can be assigned to the group so that all members of the group can access and modify the files without granting broader access to all users on the system.

The concept of ownership extends beyond simply knowing who owns a file. It involves the management of permissions based on that ownership. For example, the file owner typically has the ability to modify the file's permissions, while members of the group and others may not. In this way, ownership serves as a fundamental control mechanism in filesystem security. The owner of a file can, through their permissions, grant or restrict access to others. This ability to delegate or revoke permissions is a powerful tool for system administrators, allowing them to enforce strict security policies based on the file's content and the needs of the organization.

In addition to the basic owner and group categories, modern systems also support Access Control Lists (ACLs), which provide more granular control over file permissions. ACLs allow administrators to define permissions for specific users or groups, offering greater flexibility than the traditional owner-group-other model. With ACLs, permissions can be set for individual users or groups, regardless of whether they are the file's owner or part of the assigned group. This feature is particularly useful in complex systems where multiple users with different roles need access to various files, as it provides fine-grained control over who can do what with each file.

Managing file permissions and ownership is a vital task for system administrators, as improper settings can lead to security vulnerabilities or operational issues. For example, if sensitive files such as system configuration files or user credentials are not adequately protected, unauthorized users may gain access and compromise the system. On the other hand, overly restrictive permissions may prevent legitimate users from accessing the files they need, disrupting workflows and impeding productivity. Striking the right balance between accessibility and security requires a deep understanding of how file permissions and ownership interact within the filesystem.

In multi-user environments, it is particularly important to regularly audit file permissions and ownership to ensure they remain appropriate. Over time, permissions can become outdated as users join or leave groups, or as the system evolves. Without periodic reviews, a system's security posture may weaken, leaving files exposed or restricting access unnecessarily. Tools like chmod, chown, and ls allow administrators to view, modify, and audit file permissions and ownership, helping to maintain a secure and efficient system.

File permissions and ownership are essential concepts in managing access to data in a multi-user environment. By understanding the structure of file permissions, the roles of ownership, and the tools available to manage them, system administrators can ensure that their systems are both secure and functional. Proper management of permissions and ownership allows organizations to protect sensitive data, enable collaboration among users, and prevent unauthorized access, all while maintaining an efficient and organized system.

Filesystem Mounting and Unmounting

Filesystem mounting and unmounting are essential operations in managing a system's storage. They define how the operating system interacts with storage devices, allowing files and directories to be accessed and modified. Understanding the process of mounting and unmounting filesystems is crucial for system administrators, as it ensures that storage devices are correctly recognized and safely removed from the system. Mounting is the act of making a filesystem accessible to the operating system, while unmounting ensures that no processes are accessing the filesystem, allowing it to be safely detached from the system. These operations are integral to the proper functioning of any modern computer system, especially in multi-user environments where multiple filesystems and storage devices are often in use simultaneously.

When a filesystem is mounted, it is associated with a specific directory in the filesystem hierarchy, known as the mount point. This mount point serves as the entry point to access the files stored on the mounted filesystem. The act of mounting essentially links the physical storage device—whether it is a hard drive, solid-state drive, network storage, or other forms of media—into the logical directory structure of the operating system. Once mounted, the files and directories on the device become accessible to users and applications just like any other files in the system. The operating system communicates with the storage device through the filesystem type, such as ext4, NTFS, or FAT, which determines how data is organized and accessed.

The process of mounting is typically initiated by the system administrator or by the operating system itself during boot time. In most Unix-like systems, mounting is done through the mount command, which requires the specification of the storage device and the target mount point. For instance, to mount a device like /dev/sdb1 to the /mnt directory, the administrator would run a command like mount /dev/sdb1 /mnt. After mounting, the files and directories on the device are made available to the system and can be accessed by users with appropriate permissions. This makes mounting a fundamental operation when integrating additional storage into a system, whether adding new disks or accessing network storage.

Mounting can also be automated using configuration files, such as /etc/fstab in Linux systems. This file contains a list of storage devices and their associated mount points, along with additional options like filesystem type and mount options. By configuring this file, the system can automatically mount devices during boot, ensuring that storage is readily available when the system starts. This is particularly useful in environments where multiple storage devices need to be mounted consistently, as it eliminates the need for manual intervention each time the system is restarted.

In addition to manual and automated mounting, systems also support mounting remote filesystems over a network. Network File System (NFS) and Common Internet File System (CIFS) are two protocols commonly used for this purpose. NFS allows systems to share files over a network, enabling remote access to files stored on another system as if they were local. CIFS, on the other hand, is commonly used in Windows environments to share files and printers over a network. Mounting remote filesystems follows similar principles to local mounting, but it requires network connectivity and proper permissions to access the remote system.

Unmounting is the reverse process of mounting and is equally important. Unmounting a filesystem ensures that it is safely disconnected from the operating system, preventing data corruption and ensuring that any changes to the filesystem are properly written to the storage device. Unmounting is necessary when a device is being removed, whether it is an external hard drive, a USB stick, or a network share. If a filesystem is unmounted improperly or while it is in use, there is a risk of data loss or filesystem corruption, which can render files inaccessible or cause severe system issues.

To unmount a filesystem, the umount command is used. The syntax for unmounting is similar to that of mounting, where the user specifies either the device or the mount point. For example, running umount /mnt would unmount the filesystem mounted at /mnt. It is essential to ensure that no processes or users are accessing the filesystem before unmounting it. This can be checked using tools like lsof or fuser, which show which processes are using the filesystem. If a filesystem is in use, it may not be possible to unmount it until those processes are stopped.

In some cases, the system might prevent unmounting to avoid damaging data, especially if the device is still actively being written to.

When unmounting remote filesystems, it is important to ensure that the network connection remains stable during the unmounting process. If a network share is unmounted before the connection is properly closed, the client system may experience delays or errors in accessing the filesystem. Additionally, if unmounting a network filesystem while files are being actively modified, data could be lost or corrupted. For this reason, proper synchronization and connection management are crucial when working with remote filesystems.

Another aspect to consider when mounting and unmounting filesystems is the use of mount options. Mount options are flags that can be specified at the time of mounting to control the behavior of the filesystem. These options can affect performance, security, and other aspects of the filesystem's operation. For example, the noexec option prevents executables from being run from a mounted filesystem, adding an additional layer of security. The ro option mounts the filesystem in read-only mode, preventing any write operations. Other options, like async or sync, control how data is written to the filesystem, with sync ensuring that data is written immediately to disk, while async allows the system to write data in the background for better performance.

Filesystem mounting and unmounting are also essential when dealing with system maintenance tasks. During upgrades or system repairs, administrators may need to mount special filesystems like the root filesystem or boot filesystem. In certain recovery situations, such as when a system fails to boot, the administrator might need to mount the root filesystem from a live environment to diagnose and fix issues. In these cases, proper mounting and unmounting procedures are critical to ensure that the recovery process goes smoothly without introducing further problems.

The importance of mounting and unmounting extends beyond local systems. With the rise of virtualized environments and cloud computing, mounting and unmounting remote storage is increasingly common. Virtual machines, containers, and cloud-based applications often rely on mounted filesystems to access shared storage across distributed environments. In these scenarios, mounting and unmounting must be carefully managed to ensure that the storage remains consistent and reliable across different nodes and users.

Overall, the operations of mounting and unmounting form a cornerstone of filesystem management. These tasks are integral to the process of adding new storage to a system, accessing remote resources, or safely removing devices. By understanding how filesystems are mounted and unmounted, and the tools and commands available for these tasks, system administrators can ensure that their storage devices are integrated securely and efficiently into their systems.

Understanding Filesystem Inodes

Inodes are one of the most fundamental components of a filesystem, especially in Unix-like operating systems such as Linux. At the core of filesystem architecture, inodes are responsible for storing metadata about files, ensuring the smooth and efficient operation of file management. They play a critical role in how the system manages and organizes files, offering a unique way of handling file attributes such as ownership, permissions, timestamps, and the physical location of data blocks on disk. Understanding inodes is essential for system administrators, as it helps them navigate filesystem behavior, optimize storage, and troubleshoot potential issues.

An inode is essentially a data structure used by the filesystem to store information about a file, excluding its name or actual content. The inode contains metadata about the file, such as its owner, access permissions, size, type, and the timestamps that indicate when the file was last accessed, modified, or created. These attributes are vital for the operating system to properly manage files and ensure that users can interact with them as needed. Inodes are also responsible for managing pointers to the actual data blocks on the storage device, which store the contents of the file. When a file is created, the filesystem assigns it a unique inode, which serves as the key to access its metadata and data blocks.

The importance of inodes lies in their ability to abstract file data from the actual file name and contents. When a file is created, it is given a name that is stored in a directory entry, but the inode holds the essential information about the file. This separation allows for efficient file handling, as the operating system only needs to access the inode to retrieve metadata and find the corresponding data blocks. The inode structure thus enables the filesystem to maintain a clear distinction between the file's content and its attributes, facilitating faster access, better file management, and improved security.

Each inode contains several key elements that provide detailed information about the file it represents. These elements typically include the file's owner (a user ID), the group associated with the file (a group ID), the file's size, the number of data blocks allocated to the file, and pointers to the locations of these data blocks on the disk. The inode also holds the file's mode, which dictates its permissions and determines who can access or modify the file. Timestamps, including the time the file was last accessed, modified, or created, are also stored within the inode. Additionally, the inode tracks the number of hard links pointing to the file, which determines whether the file should be deleted from the filesystem when no more links exist.

Inodes do not store the file name. Instead, they are linked to file names through directory entries. A directory is essentially a table of filenames that map to inodes. When a user accesses a file, the operating system looks up the file name in the directory and retrieves the corresponding inode. This process of separating the file name from its metadata and content is one of the key design elements of many modern filesystems, including ext4, XFS, and others. This system allows for greater flexibility, such as enabling files to have multiple names (hard links) that all point to the same inode, and facilitates better performance in file searches and access.

When a file is created in a Unix-like system, the filesystem allocates an inode from a pool of available inodes. The inode is then populated with the appropriate metadata and assigned to the new file. In some cases, the number of available inodes may become exhausted, especially in systems with a large number of small files. When this happens, even if there is still available disk space, no more files can be created unless more inodes are allocated. This situation can be avoided by carefully planning the filesystem's inode allocation when formatting a disk, ensuring that the number of inodes is sufficient for the expected workload.

The number of inodes is set when a filesystem is created, and once the filesystem is formatted, the total number of inodes is fixed. This means that the only way to increase the number of inodes is to reformat the filesystem. The inode allocation strategy determines how many inodes are created per unit of disk space, and this decision can impact performance and storage efficiency. For example, if a filesystem is expected to store many small files, a higher inode-to-disk-space ratio may be beneficial, as it ensures enough inodes are available. Conversely, for systems that will store larger files, fewer inodes may be sufficient, as large files use fewer inodes to manage their data blocks.

One of the challenges with inodes is dealing with inode fragmentation. Fragmentation occurs when inodes are spread out across the disk, rather than being stored contiguously. This can lead to performance issues, as the filesystem may need to perform additional seeks to access all the inodes. To prevent this, modern filesystems like ext4 and XFS employ strategies to reduce inode fragmentation by allocating inodes in a manner that keeps them close to the data blocks they reference. Additionally, these filesystems can dynamically allocate inodes as needed, improving efficiency in systems with varied workloads.

Inodes are also essential for ensuring the integrity of the filesystem. Since inodes store critical information about files, such as their location on disk, the integrity of inodes directly impacts the reliability of the filesystem. Filesystem integrity checks, such as those performed by fsck (file system check) tools, often involve scanning inodes to ensure that they correctly point to valid data blocks. If an inode becomes corrupted or points to invalid data blocks, it can lead to file corruption or data loss. For this reason, many filesystems employ journaling techniques to protect inode structures, ensuring that any changes to the filesystem are recorded in a journal before they are applied. This helps prevent corruption in the event of a system crash or unexpected shutdown.

The role of inodes extends beyond local filesystems. In distributed or networked environments, where files may be stored across multiple devices or systems, inodes play an important role in managing file consistency and access control. Distributed filesystems, such as NFS or Ceph, maintain their own inode structures, allowing them to track file metadata across multiple storage nodes. This ensures that files remain accessible and consistent, even in complex storage configurations.

In summary, inodes are an integral part of filesystem management, serving as the foundation for file metadata, data block location, and access control. They allow filesystems to operate efficiently by separating file names from their underlying data, offering flexibility in file management and storage. Understanding how inodes function and how they interact with the rest of the filesystem is crucial for system administrators, as it helps optimize storage, troubleshoot issues, and ensure the integrity of the system. Through careful inode management and an understanding of their structure, administrators can maintain a well-functioning and reliable filesystem.

Journaling vs Non-Journaling Filesystems

When managing a computer system, one of the most critical decisions administrators face is selecting an appropriate filesystem. A key distinction between different types of filesystems is whether they are journaling or non-journaling. This difference influences the way the filesystem handles data integrity, particularly in the event of a system crash or power failure. Journaling filesystems, as the name suggests, use a journal to keep track of changes before they are actually applied to the main filesystem. Non-journaling filesystems, on the other hand, lack this feature and rely on different mechanisms to maintain integrity. Understanding the characteristics, advantages, and trade-offs between these two types of filesystems is essential for choosing the right solution based on system requirements, data reliability needs, and performance considerations.

A journaling filesystem records changes to data in a special area called the journal or log before they are committed to the main filesystem. The journal acts as a buffer, temporarily storing metadata changes or, in some cases, full data changes before they are written to disk. By keeping a record of these operations, the filesystem can ensure that in the event of a failure—such as a system crash or power loss—the filesystem can be restored to a consistent state. This mechanism helps to avoid corruption of data and minimizes the chances of file system inconsistencies. In the event of an abrupt shutdown, the system can replay the journal to apply all the changes that were being made before the failure occurred, ensuring that the filesystem is either left in a consistent state or reverted to a previous safe state.

The key benefit of journaling is its ability to maintain the integrity of the filesystem. By keeping a log of all changes, the system can recover from crashes more quickly and safely. This feature is particularly important for systems that need to ensure high availability and minimize downtime, such as databases, enterprise servers, and other critical applications. In journaling filesystems, even if the system crashes in the middle of a write operation, the journal can provide enough information to complete the operation when the system is restarted. Common examples of journaling filesystems include ext3, ext4, NTFS, and XFS.

Journaling filesystems come in different modes, depending on how they handle data and metadata logging. Some file systems only log metadata changes, such as file names, directory structures, and permissions. This mode is known as "metadata journaling" and is faster because it only tracks changes to the file system structure, not the actual file content. However, this also means that in the event of a failure, it is possible for data to be left in an inconsistent state, as the actual file contents may not have been written to disk. Other file systems, such as the more advanced version of ext4, can perform "data journaling," where both metadata and file contents are written to the journal. While this provides greater data integrity, it also incurs a performance penalty because it requires writing more information to the journal before making changes to the filesystem.

On the other hand, non-journaling filesystems do not maintain a journal to track changes before they are written to disk. Instead, they rely on techniques such as file system consistency checks to ensure data integrity. When a system using a non-journaling filesystem crashes, it may be necessary to run a file system check (fsck) after reboot to ensure that the filesystem is consistent and that no data corruption has occurred. This process involves scanning the filesystem for inconsistencies, such as missing or orphaned blocks, and attempting to repair them. While fsck can help to recover from crashes, it is not as fast or as reliable as the journaling mechanism, as it requires more time to perform the scan and repair operations.

Non-journaling filesystems are typically simpler and faster than journaling filesystems, particularly for smaller workloads where the added overhead of journaling is not necessary. They can be more efficient in environments where data integrity is less critical, and the risk of data corruption due to sudden crashes is minimal. Non-journaling filesystems may also have a smaller performance impact when writing data, as they do not have to maintain an additional journal, making them ideal for use cases where write performance is the primary concern, such as embedded systems or certain types of temporary storage.

Despite their performance advantages, non-journaling filesystems come with notable risks. In the event of a power failure or crash, there is a higher likelihood of data corruption, as the system has no journal to fall back on for consistency. This can lead to significant issues, particularly in environments where uptime and data reliability are critical. Files may become corrupted, and in some cases, the entire filesystem may become unreadable, requiring a lengthy and sometimes incomplete recovery process. Additionally, because non-journaling filesystems rely on fsck for recovery, systems may experience downtime as the filesystem is scanned and repaired, which can be time-consuming and disrupt operations.

One advantage of non-journaling filesystems is that they tend to be simpler and easier to manage. The absence of journaling mechanisms reduces the complexity of the filesystem, which can make it easier for system administrators to diagnose issues and perform maintenance tasks. Furthermore, the lack of journaling may result in faster file system mount times, as there is no need to replay or check a journal. This can be beneficial in scenarios where quick access to storage is required after rebooting, and the overhead of journaling would not be justified.

Another important consideration is the role of the underlying hardware in determining the choice between journaling and non-journaling filesystems. On systems with modern hardware that includes high-speed storage devices, such as solid-state drives (SSDs), the performance penalty of journaling may be less noticeable. However, on older systems or those with spinning hard drives, the additional write operations required for journaling can lead to a more significant impact on performance. In these cases, a non-journaling filesystem may be preferred if the risk of data loss is deemed manageable or if data integrity is not a critical concern.

Ultimately, the choice between journaling and non-journaling filesystems depends on the specific needs of the system. Journaling filesystems are ideal for systems that prioritize data integrity, recovery speed, and reliability, while non-journaling filesystems may be more appropriate in situations where performance is the primary concern, and data consistency risks are minimal. For high-availability systems, databases, and critical applications, journaling filesystems are often the preferred option, as they offer robust protection against unexpected shutdowns. In less demanding environments, where performance outweighs the need for data protection, non-journaling filesystems may provide a simpler, faster alternative. Understanding the strengths and weaknesses of each type is essential for making an informed decision that best meets the requirements of the system.

Filesystem Compression Techniques

Filesystem compression is a technique used to reduce the amount of disk space occupied by data stored on a filesystem. It works by applying compression algorithms to files or entire filesystems, allowing more data to be stored in the same physical space. As data storage needs continue to grow, and with the increasing availability of high-speed processors and large storage devices, compression has become an important tool for system administrators seeking to optimize storage usage and improve system performance. By understanding how filesystem compression works and the different techniques available, system administrators can make informed decisions on how best to implement compression in their environments.

Compression can be applied to individual files or across entire filesystems, depending on the needs of the system. The primary goal of compression is to minimize storage space usage without significantly affecting performance. This is particularly important in systems with limited disk space or in environments where large volumes of data need to be stored efficiently, such as in virtualized environments, cloud storage, or archival systems. By reducing the amount of physical space needed to store data, compression techniques help lower costs and enhance data management efficiency.

There are two main types of compression techniques used in filesystems: lossless and lossy. Lossless compression algorithms ensure that no data is lost during the compression process. The original data can be perfectly reconstructed when decompressed. This is crucial for many filesystem applications, where data integrity is paramount, and no loss of information can be tolerated. Lossy compression, on the other hand, sacrifices some data in exchange for higher compression ratios. This type of compression is typically used in media files, such as images, audio, and video, where some loss of quality is acceptable in exchange for reducing file sizes. For filesystem compression, lossless techniques are the standard since they preserve the integrity of files.

One of the most commonly used compression techniques in modern filesystems is the use of transparent or inline compression. In transparent compression, files are automatically compressed and decompressed by the filesystem as they are read from or written to disk, without requiring any additional user intervention. This type of compression is typically seamless, with users and applications interacting with the filesystem as if the files were uncompressed. The filesystem handles the compression and decompression operations in the background, allowing for more efficient use of storage without sacrificing user experience or system performance.

There are several well-known compression algorithms used in filesystem compression, each with its advantages and trade-offs. One of the most widely used algorithms is the Zlib compression library, which is used in many filesystems and applications. Zlib is a lossless data compression library that provides a good balance between compression ratio and speed, making it suitable for a wide range of applications. It is particularly well-suited for systems that require fast compression and decompression speeds, such as in virtualized environments or systems that need to handle large amounts of data quickly. Zlib is commonly used in filesystems like Btrfs, which offers built-in support for compression.

Another compression technique commonly employed in filesystems is the LZ4 algorithm. LZ4 is known for its high speed, making it a good choice for real-time compression needs. While it may not offer the highest compression ratio compared to other algorithms, its ability to compress and decompress data very quickly makes it useful in environments where speed is the primary concern. LZ4 is often used in applications where performance is more important than achieving the maximum compression ratio, such as in high-performance computing environments or when working with large datasets that need to be accessed frequently.

In addition to Zlib and LZ4, other algorithms like Bzip2 and LZMA are also used in filesystem compression. Bzip2 provides higher compression ratios than Zlib and LZ4, but it is slower to compress and decompress data. This makes Bzip2 suitable for applications where storage efficiency is more important than speed, such as in backup and archival systems where data is written less frequently but must be stored for long periods. LZMA, which is used in the 7-Zip compression tool, offers an even higher compression ratio than Bzip2 but with even slower compression and decompression speeds. As a result, LZMA is typically used in situations where achieving the best possible compression ratio is the priority, and performance can be sacrificed.

Some modern filesystems, such as Btrfs and ZFS, include built-in support for compression. These filesystems allow system administrators to enable compression on a per-volume or per-file basis, offering a flexible approach to managing storage. Btrfs, for example, allows users to choose between different compression algorithms, such as Zlib or LZ4, depending on their needs. This level of customization enables administrators to tailor compression settings to the specific requirements of their workloads, whether they prioritize speed or storage efficiency.

Compression techniques in filesystems are not without their challenges. One of the primary concerns when implementing compression is the potential impact on performance. While compression can save significant amounts of disk space, it can also introduce overhead, as data must be compressed before it is written to disk and decompressed when it is read. The speed at which these operations occur is heavily dependent on the compression algorithm used, as well as the system's hardware capabilities. For example, a system with a powerful CPU and large amounts of memory may handle compression and decompression tasks more efficiently than a system with limited resources. For this reason, it is important to carefully consider the hardware environment when deciding whether to implement compression and which algorithm to use.

Another potential issue with filesystem compression is the risk of fragmentation. When data is compressed, it takes up less space on the disk, but as files are modified, they may become fragmented, leading to inefficiencies in storage. Some modern filesystems, like Btrfs and ZFS, have built-in mechanisms to handle fragmentation and optimize the storage of compressed data. However, in other cases, additional tools may be required to manage fragmentation effectively and maintain optimal storage performance.

Filesystem compression also has implications for data recovery. In the event of data loss or corruption, compressed files may be more difficult to recover than uncompressed files. Since the compression algorithm alters the file's structure, data recovery tools may struggle to properly decompress and recover the original file. However, many modern filesystems include built-in features like snapshots and checksumming to mitigate this risk and improve data integrity during the recovery process.

Despite these challenges, filesystem compression remains a powerful tool for optimizing storage. In environments where storage space is at a premium, or where large amounts of data need to be archived, compression can provide substantial benefits. With the right choice of algorithm and careful management of system resources, administrators can implement filesystem compression that balances space savings with performance considerations, ultimately leading to more efficient and cost-effective data management.

Filesystem Encryption Methods

Filesystem encryption is a critical method for protecting sensitive data stored on a system. In today's increasingly digital world, where cyber threats are ever-present, encryption provides a vital layer of security that ensures the confidentiality and integrity of data. It works by converting data into an unreadable format using cryptographic algorithms, and only those with the appropriate decryption keys can access the original content. This method is especially important for businesses, government agencies, and individuals who handle confidential or proprietary information. By understanding the various encryption methods available for filesystems, system administrators can better protect their systems and data from unauthorized access.

One of the most fundamental approaches to filesystem encryption is full disk encryption (FDE), which encrypts an entire disk, including the operating system, applications, and user files. Full disk encryption protects data at rest, meaning that data is secured when it is not in active use. FDE prevents unauthorized access to data by encrypting all the data stored on a device. Even if a malicious actor gains physical access to a machine, they would not be able to read the encrypted data without the correct encryption key or password. This is particularly useful for laptops, external drives, and other portable devices that may be lost or stolen. A popular example of FDE is BitLocker, a Microsoft encryption tool that is integrated into the Windows operating system. BitLocker uses the Advanced Encryption Standard (AES) algorithm to provide strong encryption for the entire drive. Similarly, macOS uses FileVault to provide full disk encryption on Apple devices, also utilizing AES.

Another widely used encryption method is the encryption of specific files or directories. This method is more selective than full disk encryption and allows administrators to encrypt only certain files or folders that need protection. This approach is particularly useful in environments where only certain types of data are sensitive or require additional layers of protection. File-based encryption can be applied to individual files without affecting the entire system, making it a more flexible option. The advantage of this method is that it provides encryption where needed without introducing the overhead of encrypting the entire filesystem. Tools like GNU Privacy Guard (GPG) or OpenSSL can be used to encrypt specific files using various algorithms such as RSA or AES. These tools allow users to create encrypted containers or encrypted volumes, which store sensitive data in a protected format while leaving other data unencrypted for performance reasons.

One of the most important concepts in filesystem encryption is the key management process. Encryption keys are required to both encrypt and decrypt data, and managing these keys securely is crucial to the overall effectiveness of the encryption system. A weak key management process can compromise the security of the entire encryption system. In full disk encryption systems, the encryption key is often stored in a secure area on the disk or on a trusted hardware device. For example, with BitLocker, the encryption key may be stored in the Trusted Platform Module (TPM), a dedicated hardware chip designed to securely store cryptographic keys. In other cases, keys may be managed remotely or backed up to a secure key server. However, if an attacker can gain access to these keys, the encryption can be bypassed, making it essential to use strong password policies and multi-factor authentication for key management.

Another method of filesystem encryption is the use of transparent encryption. Transparent encryption automatically encrypts and decrypts data without requiring user intervention. This type of encryption is often employed at the filesystem level, meaning that the operating system handles the encryption and decryption of files on-the-fly as they are read from and written to disk. The user does not need to be aware that the data is encrypted, as the process occurs seamlessly in the background. This can be especially beneficial in environments where security is a priority but where the users should not be burdened with manually managing encryption keys or passwords. Filesystems such as ZFS and Btrfs support transparent encryption, allowing system administrators to implement encryption across entire volumes or on a per-file basis. Transparent encryption solutions can be particularly useful for organizations that want to enforce encryption without requiring extensive changes to the user experience or application code.

There is also the option of using encryption at the block device level, which provides a method of encrypting data stored on a disk block by block, rather than file by file. This approach is typically used when encrypting external storage devices or partitions. Block-level encryption is more granular and provides better control over the encryption process, as it operates at a lower level within the filesystem. Logical Volume Manager (LVM) on Linux, for example, allows system administrators to create encrypted volumes on a per-partition basis. When a block-level encryption method is used, the entire block is encrypted, which can result in more efficient data protection, as the encryption and decryption processes can be performed more quickly than with file-based methods. However, block-level encryption may not be as flexible as file-based encryption, as it does not offer the same granularity of control over specific files or directories.

While filesystem encryption provides an important layer of security, it also comes with some performance overhead. The encryption and decryption processes require computational resources, which can slow down system performance, especially when working with large amounts of data. The impact on performance depends on several factors, including the encryption algorithm used, the hardware capabilities of the system, and the type of encryption (whether full disk, file-based, or block-level). Modern processors with hardware support for encryption can help reduce the performance impact, but in high-performance environments, administrators must balance the need for security with the desire for optimal performance.

Additionally, administrators need to consider the challenges of securely storing encryption keys. If the keys are lost or compromised, the encrypted data will be inaccessible. This makes proper backup and recovery procedures essential for any system employing filesystem encryption. Secure key management solutions, such as hardware security modules (HSMs) or dedicated key management servers, are often used to mitigate the risk of key loss or theft. Multi-factor authentication and access control mechanisms are also critical to ensure that only authorized users can access the encryption keys.

Data protection laws and regulations, such as the General Data Protection Regulation (GDPR) in Europe, require organizations to implement strong data protection measures, including encryption, to safeguard sensitive data. For many businesses, implementing filesystem encryption is not only a matter of security but also a legal and regulatory requirement. The encryption of personal, financial, or confidential data helps ensure that even if an attacker gains access to a storage device, the data remains unreadable and secure.

Ultimately, the choice of filesystem encryption method depends on the specific needs and risks of the system. Full disk encryption provides robust protection for data at rest, while file-based and block-level encryption offer more granular control. Transparent encryption solutions allow for seamless implementation of encryption without user intervention, and key management is a critical consideration for ensuring the security of encrypted data. By understanding the various encryption techniques available and their respective trade-offs, system administrators can select the most appropriate encryption solution to protect their systems and meet security, compliance, and performance requirements.

Managing Disk Quotas in Filesystems

Disk quotas are a critical aspect of managing file systems in multi-user environments. They provide a way to enforce limits on the amount of disk space that users or groups can consume on a system. Disk quotas are particularly useful in environments where resources are shared among many users, such as in large organizations, educational institutions, or data centers. Without quotas, users may consume excessive amounts of disk space, potentially impacting system performance and affecting other users. Managing disk quotas ensures that disk resources are allocated efficiently and that the system remains stable and responsive. By understanding how disk quotas work and how to configure them, system administrators can better manage storage resources, prevent abuse, and ensure fair usage across all users.

At its core, a disk quota is a limit that restricts how much disk space a user or group can use. Quotas can be set on a per-user or per-group basis and are applied to file systems that support them, such as ext4, XFS, or ZFS. These limits are typically enforced at the filesystem level, meaning that they apply regardless of the type of files being stored. Disk quotas work by monitoring the number of disk blocks or inodes a user or group consumes. A block is a unit of storage on a disk, typically ranging from 4 KB to several megabytes, depending on the filesystem's block size. An inode is a data structure used to store information about a file, and it plays an important role in the management of file storage. By controlling both the amount of disk space and the number of inodes users can use, disk quotas provide a comprehensive approach to managing storage resources.

There are two main types of disk quotas: soft and hard quotas. A soft quota is a temporary limit that a user or group can exceed for a certain period of time, while a hard quota is a strict, unchangeable limit that cannot be exceeded under any circumstances. Soft quotas allow users some flexibility in managing their disk usage, while hard quotas are used to enforce strict limits that ensure users do not consume more than their fair share of storage. System administrators typically set soft quotas with a grace period, allowing users to exceed the limit for a specific amount of time before they are required to reduce their usage. If users exceed their hard quota, they will be unable to create new files or modify existing ones until they free up space or the quota is increased. This dual-approach allows administrators to balance flexibility with enforcement, depending on the needs of the system.

To manage disk quotas effectively, administrators must configure the system to track disk usage. This involves enabling quota support within the filesystem and setting up the appropriate tools for monitoring and enforcing limits. In many Linux-based systems, the quota command is used to manage disk quotas. To enable quotas on a filesystem, administrators typically need to mount the filesystem with the usrquota or grpquota options, which enable user or group quota tracking, respectively. Once enabled, administrators can use the edquota command to set soft and hard limits on the amount of disk space or inodes that users or groups can consume. The repquota command allows administrators to generate reports showing current disk usage and quota status for all users or groups, which is helpful for monitoring and auditing purposes.

Effective disk quota management requires administrators to set appropriate limits based on the needs of the organization and the system's workload. For example, in environments where users are likely to generate large files, such as video editing or scientific computing environments, quotas should be set higher to accommodate these needs. On the other hand, in environments where users are storing smaller files, such as in an office setting, quotas may need to be set lower to prevent any single user from consuming too much space. Balancing quotas for different user groups helps ensure that the system remains fair and equitable, with each user receiving an appropriate amount of storage.

In addition to managing disk space usage, administrators must also consider inode quotas. Inodes are used to store metadata about files, such as file names, ownership, and permissions. Each file on a filesystem consumes an inode, and in some situations, a user may run out of inodes even if they have not reached their disk space quota. This is particularly common in systems that store a large number of small files, as each file consumes an inode regardless of its size. Setting inode quotas ensures that users cannot create an excessive number of files, preventing the system from becoming overloaded with metadata. Administrators can configure inode quotas similarly to disk space quotas, using the same tools and commands to track and limit inode usage.

Monitoring disk quota usage is essential for maintaining a healthy filesystem. System administrators can use various tools to track how much space or how many inodes users are consuming. In Linux systems, the quota command provides a quick overview of a user's current disk usage, including both the space consumed and the number of inodes used. The repquota command, as mentioned earlier, is useful for generating reports on disk usage for all users or groups, helping administrators identify potential issues before they become critical. Additionally, many systems have automated tools that can send alerts when users approach their quota limits, helping to prevent disruptions and ensure that users are aware of any space constraints.

While disk quotas provide an essential tool for managing system resources, they also come with some challenges. One challenge is ensuring that quotas are set appropriately for different types of users. For example, setting quotas too low for a user who requires large amounts of storage can lead to frustration and decreased productivity. On the other hand, setting quotas too high can lead to inefficient use of disk space, which may negatively impact other users. As a result, administrators must carefully consider the needs of each user or group and set quotas accordingly. Periodically reviewing and adjusting quotas is also important to ensure that they remain relevant as storage needs evolve.

Another challenge is handling quota enforcement during high-demand periods. In some cases, users may need additional disk space temporarily, such as when working on a large project or storing backups. Administrators can adjust quotas on a temporary basis to accommodate these needs, but this must be done with caution to avoid disrupting the fairness of the system. Grace periods and soft quotas help address this issue by giving users the flexibility to exceed their limits for short periods without immediately blocking access to the filesystem. However, administrators must carefully monitor these exceptions to ensure they do not become permanent.

In large-scale environments, automating quota management can help reduce administrative overhead. Many modern systems allow for the automatic creation of quotas when new user accounts are created, or they provide automated tools for adjusting quotas based on usage patterns. Automation can save time and ensure that quotas are consistently applied across the system, reducing the risk of human error and improving overall system efficiency.

Overall, managing disk quotas is a vital part of filesystem administration, especially in multi-user environments where resources need to be allocated fairly and efficiently. By setting appropriate disk space and inode limits, monitoring usage, and adjusting quotas as needed, system administrators can ensure that the filesystem remains stable and that users have access to the resources they need without overburdening the system. Disk quotas provide a powerful mechanism for maintaining order and efficiency in systems with limited storage, helping to prevent disk space exhaustion and ensuring a fair distribution of resources among users.

Filesystem Performance Tuning

Filesystem performance tuning is an essential aspect of system administration, particularly for environments where storage efficiency and data access speeds are crucial. In many systems, the performance of the filesystem can have a significant impact on overall system responsiveness, application performance, and user experience. Performance tuning involves adjusting various parameters and settings to optimize the efficiency of the filesystem, ensuring it can handle the workloads placed on it effectively. The process requires a deep understanding of how filesystems work, the types of workloads they support, and how the underlying hardware interacts with the software. By understanding these elements, administrators can tweak the system to meet the specific needs of their environment.

One of the first aspects to consider when tuning filesystem performance is understanding the type of workload the system is handling. For example, systems that handle a large number of small files, such as web servers or email servers, may benefit from different tuning strategies than systems that manage large files, such as video editing platforms or databases. Filesystem performance can be influenced by various factors, including read and write patterns, file sizes, access frequencies, and the type of storage devices in use. Optimizing the filesystem for a specific workload ensures that the system operates efficiently and that resources are allocated appropriately.

The underlying hardware on which the filesystem resides plays a crucial role in its performance. Disk speed, whether from hard disk drives (HDDs) or solid-state drives (SSDs), directly impacts how quickly data can be read from and written to the filesystem. SSDs are significantly faster than HDDs, and modern filesystems can be tuned to take advantage of these faster devices. For example, systems using SSDs may benefit from larger block sizes, as the faster read and write speeds of SSDs make handling larger chunks of data more efficient. In contrast, HDDs tend to perform better with smaller block sizes, as they require less mechanical movement to access the data. Adjusting block sizes according to the type of storage medium can help improve overall filesystem performance.

Another important factor in filesystem performance tuning is disk caching. Filesystems rely heavily on caching to speed up access to frequently used data. Caching mechanisms store copies of frequently accessed files in memory or in a dedicated cache on the storage device itself. This reduces the need for the system to repeatedly read from disk, which can be time-consuming. Filesystems like ext4, XFS, and ZFS implement various caching techniques to improve read and write speeds. Tuning these cache parameters, such as adjusting the cache size or the eviction policy, can improve performance, particularly in systems with high read/write demands. However, there is a balance to be struck, as allocating too much memory for caching can lead to performance issues in other areas of the system, such as application processes or system stability.

Another way to optimize filesystem performance is by minimizing fragmentation. Fragmentation occurs when data is scattered across different parts of the disk, leading to inefficient storage and slower access times. While modern filesystems like ext4 and XFS are designed to minimize fragmentation, it can still occur over time, especially in systems that frequently create, delete, and modify files. Defragmenting the filesystem or periodically optimizing the file layout can help maintain high performance. In some cases, filesystems like ZFS can automatically optimize the layout of files to reduce fragmentation, which helps maintain consistent performance over time. Monitoring fragmentation levels and taking steps to address it proactively can ensure that the filesystem performs optimally in the long run.

Filesystem performance can also be influenced by the way in which data is accessed. For example, sequential reads and writes, where data is accessed in a continuous stream, generally perform better than random accesses, where data is spread out across the disk. This is particularly true for traditional spinning hard drives. For systems that involve heavy random access, such as databases or file servers, tuning the filesystem to handle random I/O more efficiently can improve performance. One technique for improving performance in such environments is to use a filesystem that is optimized for handling large amounts of random I/O, such as XFS, which offers high scalability and low-latency performance. Additionally, using a filesystem with support for journaling can help ensure data consistency while also improving I/O performance during write operations.

In environments where performance is critical, it may be necessary to adjust filesystem settings to prioritize speed over other factors such as data integrity or redundancy. For instance, disabling certain features like data checksumming or write barriers can improve write performance, but it comes at the expense of increased risk in the event of a crash or power failure. Write barriers ensure that write operations are completed in the correct order, preventing data corruption. However, for certain use cases where performance is prioritized over safety, administrators may choose to disable these features. This approach is commonly used in high-performance computing environments, where speed is the most important factor, and the likelihood of data corruption is minimal.

One of the more advanced techniques for tuning filesystem performance is through the use of filesystem-specific mount options. Mount options allow administrators to configure various filesystem parameters at the time the filesystem is mounted. For example, in Linux-based systems, mount options like noatime and nodiratime can be used to disable updating the access time for files and directories, which reduces the amount of write activity on the filesystem. This can be particularly useful in environments with high read loads, such as web servers, where minimizing unnecessary writes can improve performance. Similarly, options like data=writeback in ext4 or XFS allow for more aggressive caching of write operations, potentially improving write performance but at the cost of immediate data consistency.

Another method of improving filesystem performance is the use of storage-tiering. Storage-tiering involves using different types of storage devices with varying performance characteristics and automatically placing data on the most appropriate tier based on usage patterns. For example, frequently accessed data can be stored on fast SSDs, while less frequently accessed data can be stored on slower, higher-capacity HDDs. Filesystems like ZFS and Btrfs support storage-tiering features, allowing administrators to configure policies that move data between storage tiers based on access patterns or data age. This can lead to significant performance improvements, especially in systems with large amounts of data that exhibit varying access frequencies.

Finally, regular monitoring and analysis of filesystem performance are crucial for maintaining optimal system operation. Tools such as iotop, iostat, and blktrace can help administrators monitor disk I/O performance in real-time, identifying any bottlenecks or performance issues. By analyzing these metrics and adjusting filesystem parameters accordingly, administrators can proactively address performance degradation before it affects the system. Additionally, filesystem logs and system performance logs can be analyzed to identify trends and areas for improvement.

In environments with heavy workloads or specific performance demands, the combination of these tuning strategies can significantly enhance filesystem performance. Each system has unique needs, and tuning the filesystem to match those needs ensures that resources are utilized efficiently. Whether adjusting cache settings, optimizing data access patterns, or choosing the right filesystem for the workload, careful performance tuning plays a pivotal role in ensuring a system operates smoothly and efficiently.

Tools for Filesystem Diagnostics

Filesystem diagnostics play an essential role in ensuring the integrity, performance, and overall health of storage systems. Effective diagnostic tools allow system administrators to monitor filesystems, detect issues, and troubleshoot problems before they escalate into more significant failures. Given that modern filesystems are complex and often house vast amounts of data, being able to quickly and efficiently assess the health of a filesystem is critical. With the right tools, administrators can identify corrupted files, check for performance bottlenecks, and ensure that the filesystem is functioning as expected. These tools are an invaluable part of routine system maintenance and are often the first line of defense when diagnosing filesystem-related issues.

One of the primary tools used in filesystem diagnostics is the fsck command, short for file system consistency check. It is commonly used in Unix-like operating systems, such as Linux and macOS, to check and repair filesystems. The fsck utility scans the filesystem for errors, such as corrupted metadata or missing inodes, and attempts to repair them. When a system is rebooted or when a filesystem is unmounted improperly, fsck can be used to perform an integrity check to ensure that no data is lost and that the filesystem is in a consistent state. The tool can be run manually by administrators or set up to run automatically during system boot. Depending on the severity of the issue, fsck can fix minor issues such as fixing orphaned blocks or correcting filesystem metadata, or it may require more intensive repairs for serious problems like damaged superblocks.

In addition to fsck, many Linux distributions offer other diagnostic tools that help assess filesystem health. For example, the dmesg command is commonly used to display system messages, including logs related to filesystem operations. dmesg can show useful information about errors or warnings that may have occurred during filesystem access, such as read/write failures or disk errors. This tool is particularly useful for diagnosing hardware issues that might affect the filesystem, such as a failing disk or connectivity issues with a storage device. By checking the dmesg output, administrators can quickly identify if a disk failure is causing issues within the filesystem.

Another key tool for filesystem diagnostics is smartctl, which interfaces with the SMART (Self-Monitoring, Analysis, and Reporting Technology) system built into many modern hard drives and solid-state drives. smartctl allows administrators to check the health status of a disk, including metrics such as temperature, error rates, and the overall health of the drive. By running smartctl, administrators can detect signs of imminent hardware failure, such as increased numbers of bad sectors or an unusually high number of reallocated sectors. This is crucial for proactive system maintenance, as it helps identify failing drives before they cause data loss or filesystem corruption.

For diagnosing disk usage and identifying space issues within filesystems, the du (disk usage) and df (disk free) commands are indispensable. The df command provides a snapshot of the disk usage of mounted filesystems, displaying information about total space, used space, available space, and the filesystem's mount point. It is helpful for quickly identifying if a filesystem is running low on space, which can lead to performance degradation or even cause the system to fail to write new data. The du command, on the other hand, shows the disk usage of individual directories and files, helping administrators pinpoint which files or directories are consuming the most space. This can be particularly useful when diagnosing issues related to excessive disk usage or when looking for large, unnecessary files that can be deleted to free up space.

For performance-related diagnostics, the iostat command is commonly used. It provides information about input/output performance, showing statistics for disk usage, including the number of read and write operations, transfer rates, and response times. iostat is useful for identifying bottlenecks in the filesystem, such as excessive read/write latency or high disk utilization. By monitoring these metrics, administrators can detect when the system's disk performance is under strain, allowing them to take steps to resolve the issue, such as optimizing filesystem parameters or adding additional storage resources.

Another useful tool for diagnosing filesystem issues is blktrace, a powerful tool for tracing block-level I/O operations in Linux. It provides a detailed view of how data is being transferred to and from storage devices, allowing administrators to identify issues related to disk I/O patterns, queuing delays, or high disk contention. By analyzing the output of blktrace, administrators can gain deep insight into the performance characteristics of their storage devices and identify potential issues affecting filesystem performance. This level of detail is particularly useful in environments where disk I/O performance is critical, such as databases or high-performance computing systems.

For more in-depth analysis, the xfs_check and xfs_repair tools are specifically designed for the XFS filesystem. These tools allow administrators to check the integrity of XFS filesystems and repair any inconsistencies or corruption that may have occurred. The xfs_check tool checks the filesystem for errors, while xfs_repair attempts to fix any issues found during the check. XFS is a high-performance filesystem commonly used in enterprise environments, and having specialized tools for diagnosing and repairing XFS-specific issues ensures that the filesystem remains reliable and stable.

Similarly, the btrfs scrub command is used to check the integrity of a Btrfs filesystem. Btrfs, known for its advanced features like snapshots and checksumming, provides a built-in mechanism for detecting and repairing data corruption. The btrfs scrub command scans the filesystem for errors and automatically attempts to repair any detected issues. This is especially important for maintaining data integrity in systems that rely on Btrfs's features, such as snapshot-based backups or data redundancy.

Filesystem diagnostics also require monitoring tools that track filesystem performance and health over time. The collectd tool is a popular choice for gathering performance data from various system components, including filesystems. By collecting data such as disk usage, read/write speeds, and filesystem health metrics, collectd helps administrators spot trends and patterns in filesystem performance, making it easier to predict when maintenance or upgrades may be needed. The data collected by collectd can also be integrated into monitoring systems like Grafana or Prometheus, providing real-time insights into filesystem health and performance.

In addition to these tools, many filesystems come with their own diagnostic utilities. For instance, the ZFS filesystem includes tools like zpool status and zfs list that provide insights into the health of storage pools and datasets. These tools help administrators assess the status of ZFS filesystems, detect issues like degraded pools, and perform maintenance tasks such as scrub operations to check for corruption.

Ultimately, having a comprehensive set of diagnostic tools at hand is essential for maintaining the health and performance of a filesystem. System administrators must be proactive in using these tools to regularly check the filesystem's integrity, monitor disk usage, and optimize performance. By leveraging a combination of tools like fsck, smartctl, dmesg, iostat, and others, administrators can quickly identify and resolve potential issues before they escalate, ensuring that the filesystem operates efficiently and reliably. Regular filesystem diagnostics help maintain a healthy system, reduce downtime, and prevent data loss, all of which are critical for the smooth operation of any IT infrastructure.

Handling Filesystem Corruption

Filesystem corruption is a serious issue that can lead to data loss, system crashes, and decreased system performance. It occurs when the integrity of the filesystem is compromised, usually due to power failures, hardware malfunctions, software bugs, or improper system shutdowns. When a filesystem becomes corrupted, the operating system can no longer properly access or manage the files, leading to potential disruptions. Understanding how to handle filesystem corruption is essential for system administrators to mitigate damage, recover data, and restore the system to a functional state. This chapter explores the causes of filesystem corruption, the symptoms of an affected system, and the tools and techniques used to repair and recover corrupted filesystems.

One of the primary causes of filesystem corruption is an unexpected system shutdown. If the power goes out or the system crashes while files are being written to disk, the filesystem can become inconsistent. This is because the system may not have had the opportunity to flush all changes to the disk, leaving part of the filesystem in a partially written state. This can lead to missing data, broken links, or corrupted files. For example, if a file is being written when a crash occurs, the filesystem may end up with only a partial version of the file, making it unreadable. In some cases, if the system is unable to recover the corrupted data automatically, the affected files may be lost forever.

Hardware issues can also contribute to filesystem corruption. Faulty hard drives, bad sectors, or failing solid-state drives can lead to data corruption. A disk with bad sectors may not be able to read or write data correctly, which can lead to incomplete or corrupt files. Similarly, disk controllers or cables that are malfunctioning may cause data transmission errors, resulting in corrupt files. While modern filesystems like ext4 and ZFS have built-in mechanisms to detect and correct certain types of errors, hardware failures can still introduce corruption that the filesystem cannot automatically fix.

Software bugs and issues with the operating system or file management software can also cause filesystem corruption. For example, an issue in the kernel, a bug in the filesystem driver, or a flaw in the application writing to the filesystem could lead to improper handling of file operations, causing the filesystem to become inconsistent. In these cases, the problem may be due to a programming error or incompatibility between software versions, and addressing it may involve applying patches or updating the affected software. Even filesystem utilities like disk repair tools or disk usage tools, if used incorrectly or if they encounter unforeseen errors, can contribute to corruption.

Filesystem corruption can manifest in several ways, and the symptoms often depend on the extent of the corruption. One common symptom is the inability to access files or directories, with the system displaying errors such as "file not found" or "permission denied." This may occur because the filesystem's metadata or inode structure has been compromised, preventing the operating system from locating or managing files. Another common symptom is the appearance of corrupted or missing files, where files may appear empty, unreadable, or have invalid content. In some cases, applications or the system may freeze or crash when attempting to access the affected filesystem. File operations may also become slow or unresponsive, and the system may produce frequent error messages indicating issues with disk I/O or file access.

The first step in handling filesystem corruption is to identify the extent of the damage. When corruption is suspected, administrators should check the system logs for any relevant messages. In Linux-based systems, the dmesg command is particularly useful for viewing system logs related to disk I/O errors and hardware issues. Additionally, tools like smartctl can help assess the health of the hard drive or SSD by checking for signs of failure, such as increased numbers of reallocated sectors or disk read/write errors. If the corruption is caused by a hardware failure, the issue may need to be addressed by replacing the failing hardware before proceeding with repairs.

Once the cause and extent of the corruption are identified, administrators should attempt to repair the filesystem. The most common tool used for repairing corrupted filesystems in Unix-like systems is fsck, or filesystem consistency check. The fsck tool scans the filesystem for errors and attempts to fix them by repairing corrupted inodes, fixing broken links, or restoring missing metadata. When run, fsck checks the consistency of the filesystem by comparing the filesystem's metadata against the actual data stored on the disk. If discrepancies are found, fsck will attempt to correct them. In some cases, fsck may ask the administrator for confirmation before making changes to the filesystem. It is important to run fsck on unmounted filesystems, as performing repairs on a mounted filesystem could cause further damage.

For more advanced filesystems like ZFS, zpool scrub and zfs scrub are used to repair data corruption. ZFS employs checksums to detect data corruption and offers a built-in mechanism for scrubbing, or verifying the integrity of the filesystem. When running a scrub, ZFS checks each block of data for corruption, comparing the checksums to ensure that the data is intact. If ZFS detects corrupted data, it can automatically attempt to repair the affected data using redundancy provided by the system, such as mirrored storage. This feature makes ZFS particularly resilient to data corruption, but administrators must still regularly scrub the filesystem to ensure data integrity.

In cases where fsck or other repair tools are unable to fix the corruption, administrators may need to consider more drastic measures, such as restoring from backups. A robust backup strategy is critical to mitigating the risks associated with filesystem corruption. If the corrupted data cannot be repaired or if the filesystem is beyond recovery, administrators can restore data from the most recent backup to minimize data loss. Backup systems like incremental backups, snapshots, or cloud-based backups can make it easier to restore a system to a known good state. However, in environments where real-time data consistency is required, tools like RAID or replication systems can offer redundancy to avoid total data loss in the event of corruption.

Once the filesystem has been repaired, it is important to prevent future corruption. Implementing regular disk checks, using proper shutdown procedures, and ensuring hardware reliability can help reduce the risk of filesystem corruption. Additionally, administrators should consider implementing tools that provide data integrity checks, such as ZFS's checksumming features, which can detect corruption early before it leads to significant issues. Keeping the operating system and filesystem software up to date is also crucial, as many updates include bug fixes and improvements to filesystem stability.

Handling filesystem corruption requires a combination of tools, proactive monitoring, and knowledge of the underlying causes of corruption. By understanding the symptoms, diagnosing the issue, and using the appropriate repair tools, administrators can minimize downtime and data loss caused by filesystem corruption. Moreover, by regularly maintaining the filesystem, performing backups, and ensuring hardware health, the risk of future corruption can be mitigated, leading to a more reliable and resilient system.

Managing and Monitoring Disk Space Usage

Effective management and monitoring of disk space usage are essential practices for ensuring the smooth operation and performance of a system. As storage requirements increase and systems handle larger amounts of data, it becomes increasingly important for administrators to keep track of disk space consumption and take steps to optimize storage resources. Without proper management, systems can experience performance degradation, errors, or even system crashes due to insufficient disk space. By monitoring disk usage regularly, administrators can identify potential issues before they escalate, ensuring that disk space is utilized efficiently and that users have the necessary resources for their work.

One of the first steps in managing disk space usage is to understand the storage requirements of the system and its applications. Different types of applications and workloads have varying storage needs. For instance, databases, file servers, and web servers tend to require large amounts of disk space to store data, logs, and configuration files, while other applications may not require as much space. By understanding the types of data being stored and how frequently it is accessed or modified, administrators can better allocate disk space, prioritize storage resources, and ensure that critical data is not at risk of being overwritten or lost due to space constraints.

Regularly monitoring disk usage is crucial for identifying trends in storage consumption. Over time, systems accumulate data in the form of files, logs, backups, and temporary files. Without monitoring tools in place, administrators may not be aware of rapid increases in disk usage that could indicate issues such as log file bloat or the growth of an application's data storage requirements. Disk space monitoring allows administrators to stay ahead of potential problems by providing insights into the current usage of disk space and enabling the prediction of future needs. In Linux-based systems, tools like df and du provide valuable information about disk usage and available space, allowing administrators to track usage at both the filesystem and directory levels. The df command shows disk space usage for mounted filesystems, while du provides more granular information, such as the size of individual directories or files.

For more advanced monitoring, there are a variety of system monitoring tools available, including both native tools and third-party solutions. These tools allow administrators to set up alerts that notify them when disk usage exceeds certain thresholds. For example, if a particular filesystem is approaching its capacity, an alert can be triggered to prompt action, such as cleaning up unnecessary files or expanding the filesystem. This proactive approach helps prevent system slowdowns or failures due to lack of disk space, reducing the risk of downtime and ensuring business continuity.

One of the most common issues related to disk space management is the accumulation of temporary files, logs, and caches. Many applications, services, and system processes generate temporary files during their operation. While these files are often required for the correct functioning of the application, they can accumulate over time and take up significant amounts of disk space. For example, web servers, database servers, and system logs can grow rapidly if not properly managed, leading to a situation where disk space is consumed by files that are no longer necessary. Disk space management practices such as log rotation, the regular cleaning of temporary files, and the use of cache management tools can help reduce unnecessary disk usage. Log rotation involves setting up automatic processes to archive, compress, or delete log files after a certain period, ensuring that log files do not consume excessive space.

Another important aspect of managing disk space is the efficient use of disk partitions. Proper partitioning ensures that different types of data are stored in separate areas of the disk, allowing for better organization and easier management of storage resources. For instance, placing the operating system, user files, and application data on separate partitions allows administrators to monitor each partition's usage independently, making it easier to identify which areas of the system are consuming the most space. Additionally, partitioning helps prevent one type of data, such as application logs, from filling up the entire disk and affecting other critical data. Over time, partition resizing may be necessary as storage needs grow or change. Tools like gparted or parted can be used to resize partitions and allocate space based on the system's evolving needs.

One challenge with disk space management in modern systems is the growing use of virtualized environments and cloud storage. Virtual machines and containers often have their own disk space allocations, and it can be difficult to track and manage disk usage across multiple instances. Disk usage monitoring tools that integrate with virtualization platforms like VMware, Hyper-V, or Docker are essential for tracking the disk consumption of virtualized systems. For instance, in virtualized environments, a single physical server may host multiple virtual machines, each consuming disk space, which can lead to fragmentation or inefficient use of available storage resources. Administrators must ensure that virtual disks are properly managed, resized as needed, and backed up to prevent issues with disk space in these environments.

In cloud environments, the management of disk space becomes even more complex, as storage resources are distributed across multiple servers and locations. Cloud storage solutions like Amazon S3, Google Cloud Storage, or Microsoft Azure Storage offer scalability, allowing administrators to scale storage resources based on demand. However, managing disk usage in the cloud requires careful monitoring to avoid over-provisioning or under-provisioning storage. Tools provided by cloud service providers, such as AWS CloudWatch or Google Cloud Monitoring, allow administrators to track the usage of cloud storage and set up alerts when certain thresholds are exceeded. Cloud storage solutions also often provide automatic tiering, which moves data between different storage classes based on access patterns, ensuring efficient use of available resources.

One of the most effective strategies for managing disk space is the use of data deduplication. Data deduplication is a technique that eliminates duplicate copies of data, reducing the overall amount of disk space required for storage. It is particularly useful in environments where multiple copies of the same data are stored, such as in backup systems or virtual machine environments. By identifying and eliminating duplicate data, deduplication ensures that storage resources are used more efficiently. Many modern backup and storage systems, such as NetApp and Veeam, offer built-in deduplication features that help reduce the amount of disk space consumed by redundant data.

In addition to managing disk space usage, it is equally important to regularly clean up unused or unnecessary files. This includes deleting old backups, temporary files, and unused applications. However, administrators should be careful when removing files to ensure that no critical data is accidentally deleted. Automated tools like cron jobs can be used to schedule regular cleanup tasks, making it easier to maintain optimal disk space usage over time.

Efficient management and monitoring of disk space are critical to maintaining system performance, preventing data loss, and ensuring the system operates smoothly. By using the right tools and strategies, administrators can ensure that disk space is allocated and used effectively. Regular monitoring, along with good practices such as log rotation, partitioning, deduplication, and cleanup, helps avoid disk space issues that can affect system functionality. Implementing these strategies ensures that storage resources are optimized, systems run efficiently, and administrators are able to address potential problems before they impact users or business operations.

Optimizing Filesystem Layout for Performance

Optimizing filesystem layout for performance is a crucial step in ensuring that a system operates at its full potential. The layout of a filesystem directly affects how data is organized and accessed, which in turn impacts the speed and efficiency of read and write operations. As storage requirements grow and systems handle more complex workloads, the need to fine-tune the filesystem layout becomes increasingly important. Properly designed filesystem layouts can help to reduce latency, improve throughput, and ensure that storage resources are used efficiently. System administrators must understand the characteristics of the filesystem, the hardware it runs on, and the type of workload being processed in order to design an optimal layout that meets the performance needs of the system.

One of the fundamental aspects of filesystem optimization is understanding the hardware on which the filesystem is deployed. Different storage devices, such as traditional hard disk drives (HDDs) and solid-state drives (SSDs), have distinct performance characteristics that can influence the design of the filesystem layout. HDDs are mechanical devices that rely on spinning disks to access data, which introduces latency due to seek times and rotational delays. As a result, HDDs perform best when data is stored contiguously, minimizing the movement of the read/write head. SSDs, on the other hand, have no moving parts and can access data at much higher speeds, regardless of its physical location on the disk. This means that SSDs benefit from different optimization strategies, such as adjusting block sizes and using different partitioning schemes, to fully leverage their high-speed capabilities.

In systems with HDDs, one of the primary considerations for optimizing the filesystem layout is minimizing fragmentation. Fragmentation occurs when files are split into non-contiguous blocks, causing the disk heads to move more frequently and increasing access times. Over time, fragmentation can lead to performance degradation as files become scattered across the disk. To prevent this, administrators should aim to allocate space in a way that minimizes fragmentation. This can be achieved by ensuring that files are written in a sequential manner and that there is adequate free space between files to accommodate future file growth. Filesystems like ext4, NTFS, and XFS provide features that help reduce fragmentation, but over time, periodic defragmentation may be necessary to maintain optimal performance.

For systems using SSDs, fragmentation is less of a concern due to the nature of the storage medium. However, SSDs still require careful layout optimization to maximize performance. SSDs have a limited number of program/erase (P/E) cycles, and data is written in blocks, which can become worn out after repeated writes. Therefore, when designing a filesystem layout for SSDs, it is essential to ensure that data is written evenly across the entire device to avoid excessive wear on specific blocks. One way to achieve this is by using a filesystem that supports wear leveling, such as ext4 or Btrfs. Wear leveling ensures that write operations are spread evenly across the SSD, extending the lifespan of the device. Additionally, administrators should configure the filesystem to use larger block sizes, which reduce the number of write operations needed for small files, thereby improving write performance.

Another critical aspect of optimizing filesystem layout is the choice of filesystem itself. Different filesystems offer different features that can impact performance, such as support for journaling, compression, and deduplication. Journaling filesystems, such as ext4, XFS, and NTFS, offer benefits in terms of data integrity, as they log changes before committing them to disk. However, journaling can introduce some performance overhead, especially for systems with heavy write operations. In such cases, administrators may choose to disable certain journaling features or use filesystems that offer more lightweight journaling, such as XFS, which is known for its high-performance capabilities in handling large datasets.

In high-performance environments, such as databases or data analytics applications, optimizing the filesystem layout can involve configuring the filesystem to better handle large files and high I/O throughput. For example, using a larger block size can improve the performance of applications that work with large files by reducing the number of I/O operations required to read or write the data. Conversely, for applications that generate a large number of small files, such as web servers or email systems, administrators should optimize the filesystem layout to handle small files more efficiently, possibly by adjusting inode settings or using a filesystem designed for handling large numbers of files with minimal overhead.

In addition to block size and filesystem choice, partitioning strategies also play a significant role in optimizing filesystem performance. Proper partitioning allows administrators to allocate resources more efficiently and isolate critical workloads. For instance, separating the operating system, user data, and application files onto different partitions can prevent one type of data from affecting the performance of others. It also provides better control over space usage and improves backup and restore processes, as each partition can be managed independently. In large-scale systems, administrators may consider using Logical Volume Manager (LVM) or similar tools to create flexible partitioning schemes that can be resized dynamically as storage needs evolve. LVM allows for the creation of logical volumes that can span multiple physical disks, improving both storage capacity and performance by distributing data across different disks.

In some cases, the use of RAID (Redundant Array of Independent Disks) can further enhance filesystem performance. RAID configurations such as RAID 0 (striping) or RAID 10 (striped and mirrored) can increase read and write speeds by distributing data across multiple disks. RAID 0, for example, splits data into blocks and writes them simultaneously to multiple disks, significantly improving performance for large, sequential read and write operations. However, RAID 0 offers no redundancy, so it is typically used in environments where performance is prioritized over data protection. For environments that require both high performance and data protection, RAID 10 or RAID 5 can be more suitable, offering a balance between speed and redundancy.

Another key consideration when optimizing filesystem layout is the use of caching mechanisms. Filesystems often rely on caching to speed up read and write operations by storing frequently accessed data in memory. Properly configuring cache settings can improve performance, particularly in systems that handle a large number of small, random read/write operations. Some filesystems, such as ZFS, provide advanced caching mechanisms, including hybrid caching, which combines both in-memory and on-disk caches to further optimize performance. Administrators should ensure that the filesystem's cache size is appropriate for the system's workload, as allocating too much memory to the cache can cause other processes to run slower, while too little cache can lead to performance bottlenecks.

Finally, ongoing monitoring and tuning are crucial to maintaining optimal filesystem performance. Disk usage patterns can change over time as the system's workload evolves, so it is important to regularly monitor filesystem performance and adjust the layout accordingly. Tools like iostat, blktrace, and iotop can help administrators identify performance bottlenecks and assess the efficiency of the filesystem layout. These tools provide real-time insights into disk I/O performance, allowing administrators to adjust parameters like block sizes, partitioning schemes, and cache settings to improve performance.

Optimizing filesystem layout for performance is a multifaceted task that requires a deep understanding of the system's hardware, workload, and filesystem characteristics. By carefully designing the filesystem layout, choosing the right filesystem for the workload, configuring partitioning and caching, and leveraging tools like RAID and LVM, administrators can significantly enhance the performance of a system. Regular monitoring and tuning are also critical to ensuring that the filesystem continues to meet performance requirements as the system grows and evolves. With the right optimizations in place, systems can handle demanding workloads more efficiently, providing faster data access, reduced latency, and improved overall performance.

RAID and Its Role in Filesystem Management

RAID, or Redundant Array of Independent Disks, is a technology that combines multiple physical disk drives into one or more logical units to improve performance, data redundancy, or both. It plays a crucial role in filesystem management by providing a way to organize storage in such a way that it increases efficiency, ensures data availability, and improves fault tolerance. RAID is widely used in server environments, enterprise storage systems, and high-performance computing setups to meet the demanding requirements of modern systems that process large volumes of data. Understanding RAID and its various levels helps system administrators make informed decisions about how to configure storage, balance performance with redundancy, and maintain high system reliability.

The concept behind RAID is to leverage multiple physical disks to either increase read and write speeds, protect against data loss due to disk failure, or both. By distributing data across several drives, RAID can reduce the time it takes to read and write data, provide backup copies of data in case of failure, and optimize the overall performance of the system. Depending on the specific RAID level used, RAID configurations can deliver varying combinations of performance, redundancy, and storage capacity, with each having its own strengths and weaknesses.

RAID can be implemented in two primary ways: software RAID and hardware RAID. Software RAID is managed by the operating system, which directly controls how the data is striped or mirrored across multiple disks. This type of RAID is typically less expensive because it does not require specialized hardware but may place a greater load on the system's CPU. Hardware RAID, on the other hand, uses a dedicated RAID controller card that handles the management of the disks independently of the operating system. Hardware RAID is often preferred in high-performance or mission-critical systems because it can offload the work from the CPU, leading to better overall system performance.

RAID offers a variety of levels, each designed for different use cases. The most common RAID levels include RAID 0, RAID 1, RAID 5, and RAID 10, each with its unique configuration and benefits. RAID 0, also known as striping, splits data into chunks and writes them across multiple disks, offering improved performance by allowing simultaneous reads and writes. However, RAID 0 provides no redundancy. If one disk fails, all data is lost. RAID 1, or mirroring, duplicates data across two or more disks, ensuring that an exact copy of the data is available in the event of a disk failure. RAID 1 offers excellent data redundancy but does not provide any performance boost, as the data is simply duplicated.

RAID 5 combines the benefits of both RAID 0 and RAID 1 by using a technique called parity. Data is striped across multiple disks, like in RAID 0, but parity information is also stored on one of the disks, allowing data to be reconstructed in the event of a disk failure. RAID 5 provides a good balance between performance, redundancy, and storage efficiency, as it requires only one extra disk to store parity information. RAID 10, also known as RAID 1+0, is a combination of RAID 1 and RAID 0. It provides both redundancy and performance by mirroring data (like RAID 1) and then striping the mirrors (like RAID 0). RAID 10 offers excellent performance and redundancy but at the cost of storage efficiency, as it requires twice the number of disks to store the data.

RAID plays a significant role in filesystem management because it helps administrators balance the competing demands of speed, redundancy, and cost. In environments where data loss is not an option, such as in databases or mission-critical applications, RAID provides the necessary fault tolerance to protect against disk failures. RAID 5 and RAID 10 are often the preferred configurations in such environments, as they provide both high availability and good performance. However, even in these high-demand environments, RAID cannot replace a proper backup strategy. While RAID can protect against a single disk failure, it does not safeguard against other types of data loss, such as accidental file deletion or corruption. For this reason, RAID should be considered as part of a broader data protection strategy that includes regular backups and disaster recovery planning.

For high-performance systems, RAID configurations like RAID 0 or RAID 10 are particularly beneficial. RAID 0's ability to stripe data across multiple disks significantly improves read and write speeds, making it ideal for applications that require high throughput, such as video editing, gaming, or data analysis. RAID 10, which combines the advantages of both striping and mirroring, offers the best of both worlds: excellent read and write performance with redundancy. However, RAID 10's higher cost, as it requires double the number of disks for mirroring, may make it impractical for systems with limited budget or where storage capacity is a higher priority than performance.

RAID also plays an important role in the management of storage scalability. As data grows, it becomes necessary to expand storage capacity to meet increasing demands. Many RAID systems, particularly those using hardware RAID, offer features such as online capacity expansion or hot swapping, allowing administrators to add or replace disks without taking the system offline. This flexibility enables administrators to scale storage efficiently without interrupting system operations. The ability to expand a RAID array without downtime is particularly valuable in environments that demand high availability, such as in e-commerce, cloud services, and large-scale databases.

In addition to scaling storage, RAID also helps to optimize the use of storage resources. Through the use of advanced RAID configurations, administrators can maximize disk space usage while minimizing wasted capacity. For example, RAID 5 strikes a balance between redundancy and storage efficiency, requiring only one additional disk for parity. By using RAID 5, organizations can ensure that their data is protected while making the most efficient use of available disk space. Similarly, RAID 6, an extension of RAID 5, provides additional redundancy by using two parity blocks instead of one. This provides fault tolerance against two simultaneous disk failures, though it comes at the cost of additional storage overhead for parity data.

RAID is not without its challenges, and understanding its limitations is critical for system administrators. While RAID provides fault tolerance, it cannot guarantee data protection in all situations. For example, if multiple disks fail in a RAID 5 array, data can be lost, as the parity information may not be sufficient to reconstruct the lost data. Additionally, RAID does not protect against logical failures, such as file system corruption, malware, or human error. For this reason, RAID should always be used in conjunction with a robust backup system. Additionally, RAID configurations that involve parity calculations, such as RAID 5, can result in slower write speeds due to the overhead of generating parity data. As a result, administrators must consider the trade-offs between performance and redundancy when selecting the appropriate RAID level.

RAID continues to play a vital role in filesystem management, providing organizations with the tools to optimize performance, enhance data redundancy, and scale storage as needed. By understanding the different RAID levels and their trade-offs, administrators can tailor the storage setup to meet the specific needs of their environment. RAID ensures that data is stored efficiently and is protected against hardware failures, contributing to the overall reliability and performance of the filesystem. With the right RAID configuration, administrators can meet the ever-increasing demands for speed, capacity, and data protection in modern systems.

Software RAID vs Hardware RAID

RAID, or Redundant Array of Independent Disks, is a storage technology that combines multiple physical drives into a single logical unit to enhance performance, data redundancy, or both. This can be achieved using two primary methods: software RAID and hardware RAID. Both approaches have their distinct advantages, limitations, and appropriate use cases. While they both serve the same fundamental purpose of improving data availability and system performance, the underlying mechanisms of software RAID and hardware RAID differ significantly. Understanding these differences is essential for system administrators to make informed decisions when configuring storage solutions.

Software RAID is a type of RAID that is managed by the operating system using software-based tools. In this configuration, the CPU and system resources are responsible for managing the RAID operations, such as data striping, mirroring, and parity calculations. Software RAID is typically implemented using operating system utilities like Linux's mdadm or Windows' built-in disk management tools. Since software RAID does not require additional hardware components, it is often considered more cost-effective, especially for systems with limited budgets or those requiring only basic RAID functionality.

The primary advantage of software RAID is its flexibility. Since it is managed by the operating system, it can be configured to work with almost any type of storage hardware, as long as the necessary drivers are available. This flexibility allows administrators to create RAID arrays using standard off-the-shelf drives without needing proprietary hardware. Additionally, software RAID can support a wide variety of RAID levels, such as RAID 0, RAID 1, RAID 5, and RAID 10, depending on the system's requirements. This versatility makes it an attractive option for small-scale or non-enterprise environments where cost and flexibility are the primary concerns.

One of the key benefits of software RAID is its ability to be more easily modified and upgraded. Since it does not rely on specialized hardware, administrators can add or remove drives, change RAID levels, or even migrate data to a new storage system without being limited by hardware constraints. For example, changing the RAID level or expanding an array is simpler in software RAID because it does not require additional hardware reconfiguration or replacement. This makes software RAID an excellent choice for environments where the storage configuration is expected to evolve over time.

However, software RAID does have some disadvantages. One of the most notable drawbacks is the performance overhead. Since RAID operations are handled by the system's CPU and memory, software RAID can place a significant load on the system, especially during heavy disk I/O operations. This can lead to slower performance, particularly in environments with high transaction volumes or large datasets. The CPU's involvement in RAID processing can also introduce delays, as it has to handle other tasks simultaneously. This is particularly problematic in systems that require low-latency operations or high throughput, such as databases or high-performance computing environments. Additionally, software RAID is highly dependent on the operating system's kernel and can suffer from performance degradation if the operating system is not optimized for RAID management.

On the other hand, hardware RAID involves using a dedicated RAID controller card that offloads RAID processing from the CPU and manages the RAID array independently of the operating system. This hardware-based approach provides several advantages over software RAID. By using a dedicated RAID controller, hardware RAID can significantly improve performance, as the controller is designed specifically to handle RAID operations. The controller can perform tasks like parity calculations, data striping, and mirroring without burdening the system's main CPU, which leads to faster read and write operations. This is especially beneficial in high-performance environments that require large amounts of data to be processed quickly and efficiently.

Hardware RAID also provides additional features that are not available with software RAID. For example, many hardware RAID controllers offer built-in battery-backed cache, which ensures that write operations are not lost in the event of a power failure. This is a crucial feature for applications that require data integrity, such as databases or financial systems. Furthermore, hardware RAID often comes with advanced features such as hot-swapping of drives, which allows drives to be replaced or added without shutting down the system. This increases uptime and makes it easier to manage storage in environments where continuous availability is critical.

Another benefit of hardware RAID is the enhanced data protection it offers. Hardware RAID controllers typically support more advanced RAID levels, such as RAID 6 or RAID 60, which provide double parity and offer better fault tolerance than software RAID. These advanced levels are particularly useful in high-availability environments, where data redundancy is essential. In addition, hardware RAID controllers often include monitoring tools that allow administrators to check the status of the array, detect drive failures, and receive alerts about potential issues, providing greater control over the health of the storage system.

However, hardware RAID also has its drawbacks. One of the primary disadvantages is the cost. Hardware RAID requires a dedicated RAID controller card, which adds to the overall expense of the system. In enterprise environments, where multiple storage arrays are needed, the cost of hardware RAID can become significant. Additionally, hardware RAID is often less flexible than software RAID. The RAID controller may be proprietary, which can limit compatibility with other systems or storage devices. If the RAID controller fails, recovering data or migrating the array to a different controller can be complicated, and in some cases, it may require specialized knowledge or tools.

Another consideration with hardware RAID is the dependency on the RAID controller. While the controller provides many advantages, it can also introduce a point of failure. If the controller experiences a malfunction or if the hardware is no longer supported, it can be difficult to recover the data. Additionally, many hardware RAID controllers do not support certain RAID levels or advanced features, limiting the options available for fine-tuning the storage configuration.

The choice between software RAID and hardware RAID depends on the specific needs of the environment. For small businesses or personal systems with limited budgets, software RAID can be a viable solution. It offers flexibility and ease of management, with the added benefit of being cost-effective. For systems that require high performance, scalability, and fault tolerance, such as enterprise servers or data centers, hardware RAID is often the better choice. Its ability to offload RAID processing from the CPU and provide additional features such as battery-backed cache, hot-swapping, and advanced RAID levels makes it an ideal solution for environments where performance and data integrity are paramount.

In summary, both software RAID and hardware RAID have their distinct advantages and disadvantages. Software RAID is cost-effective, flexible, and easy to implement but can suffer from performance overhead. Hardware RAID, on the other hand, provides superior performance, additional features, and greater data protection but comes at a higher cost and offers less flexibility. By understanding the differences between these two approaches, system administrators can select the appropriate RAID solution based on the specific needs of their environment.

Using Logical Volume Manager (LVM) for Filesystems

Logical Volume Manager (LVM) is a powerful tool for managing disk storage in Linux and other Unix-like operating systems. It allows administrators to create flexible and dynamic storage configurations by abstracting the underlying physical storage devices and providing a virtualized layer of storage management. LVM enables the creation, resizing, and management of logical volumes (LVs) that act as flexible storage devices, which can be easily resized, extended, or shrunk as needed. This makes LVM an essential tool for systems where storage requirements are dynamic, such as in virtualized environments, cloud computing, or enterprise systems where flexibility and scalability are critical.

The core concept behind LVM is its ability to pool multiple physical volumes (PVs) into a single storage unit known as a volume group (VG). A physical volume is typically a disk or a partition, and by combining multiple physical volumes into a volume group, administrators can create a pool of storage that is not tied to any single physical device. This abstraction allows for greater flexibility in managing disk space and allocating storage resources without being constrained by the limitations of individual physical devices. Logical volumes are then created within the volume group, which appear as regular storage devices that can be formatted and mounted like traditional disk partitions. This setup allows administrators to easily manage disk space without worrying about the physical constraints of the underlying hardware.

One of the primary advantages of using LVM is the ability to easily resize logical volumes. With traditional partitioning schemes, resizing partitions can be complex and error-prone, often requiring repartitioning of disks, potentially resulting in data loss. LVM eliminates this problem by allowing administrators to resize logical volumes on the fly, without the need to unmount the filesystem or disrupt system operations. Whether increasing or decreasing the size of a logical volume, LVM provides a simple and safe way to allocate or release disk space. This ability to resize volumes dynamically is particularly valuable in environments with rapidly changing storage needs, such as databases or virtual machines, where storage requirements can fluctuate frequently.

Another key feature of LVM is its support for volume snapshots. A snapshot is a point-in-time copy of a logical volume that allows administrators to create backups or perform system maintenance without disrupting operations. Snapshots are often used for creating backups of live systems or to take a backup before performing risky operations like system updates or software installations. LVM snapshots are efficient because they do not create full copies of data. Instead, they track changes made to the original logical volume after the snapshot is taken, which saves disk space. When a snapshot is deleted, the changes that were tracked since its creation are discarded, ensuring that only the necessary data is retained. This makes snapshots an excellent solution for disaster recovery or testing without affecting the production environment.

LVM also supports the concept of striping and mirroring, which are essential features for improving performance and ensuring data redundancy. Striping is the process of spreading data across multiple physical volumes to improve performance. By distributing read and write operations across several disks, striping can significantly increase throughput, particularly for applications that require high disk I/O, such as video editing or database management. LVM enables striping by allowing administrators to create striped logical volumes that span multiple physical volumes. This can result in faster access to data by taking advantage of the parallelism offered by multiple disks. However, it's important to note that striping does not provide any data redundancy, meaning that if one disk in a striped volume fails, data will be lost.

To ensure data redundancy, LVM supports mirroring, which creates duplicate copies of data on different physical volumes. Mirrored logical volumes are similar to RAID 1 configurations, where data is written to two or more disks simultaneously, ensuring that if one disk fails, the data is still available on another. LVM's mirroring feature helps improve data availability and reliability, making it suitable for critical systems that cannot afford downtime or data loss. By using LVM to create mirrored logical volumes, administrators can provide fault tolerance and ensure that systems remain operational even in the event of hardware failures.

In addition to striping and mirroring, LVM provides support for volume resizing and expansion. If a system's storage requirements increase, LVM allows administrators to extend logical volumes easily by adding additional physical volumes to the volume group. This expansion process can be done without disrupting the system or requiring data migration, making LVM an excellent choice for growing systems or cloud environments where storage needs change frequently. Administrators can add new disks or storage devices to the volume group and then extend the logical volumes to take advantage of the newly available space. This flexibility enables systems to scale seamlessly, supporting large datasets or growing workloads.

LVM also provides features that improve storage efficiency. For example, the ability to allocate logical volumes on an as-needed basis ensures that space is used efficiently. Administrators can create logical volumes of varying sizes and allocate them only when needed, rather than pre-allocating fixed disk space. This helps optimize disk usage, especially in environments where storage requirements are unpredictable or where there are a large number of virtual machines or containers. By efficiently managing storage resources, LVM can help reduce the amount of unused or wasted disk space, which is particularly valuable in large-scale systems or cloud environments where maximizing storage efficiency is a priority.

While LVM offers many advantages, it is important to consider some of the challenges that come with using it. One of the primary challenges is the complexity of LVM configuration and management. Although LVM provides powerful features, administrators must have a good understanding of how it works to configure it correctly. Misconfigurations, such as incorrectly resizing logical volumes or mismanaging volume groups, can lead to data loss or system instability. Additionally, while LVM is generally reliable, issues such as disk failures or corruption within the volume group can be more complicated to resolve compared to traditional disk partitioning schemes. This makes it important for administrators to monitor LVM volumes regularly, ensure that backups are taken, and have a disaster recovery plan in place in case of failure.

LVM also requires careful management of metadata. Metadata is critical for LVM to track the mapping of logical volumes to physical volumes, as well as for operations such as resizing or creating snapshots. If metadata becomes corrupted or lost, the logical volumes may become unmanageable or data may become inaccessible. Administrators must ensure that LVM metadata is properly backed up and that the system is configured to handle failures safely.

Overall, Logical Volume Manager provides a flexible and dynamic way to manage storage in modern systems. It enables administrators to create, resize, and manage logical volumes, improving the scalability and efficiency of storage. The ability to use striping, mirroring, and snapshots makes LVM a powerful tool for optimizing performance, ensuring data redundancy, and simplifying system maintenance. By abstracting physical storage and providing a logical layer for storage management, LVM allows systems to scale seamlessly while providing the necessary tools for data protection and performance tuning. Properly configured and maintained, LVM can help ensure that a system's storage infrastructure remains flexible, efficient, and resilient in the face of growing demands.

Partitioning Strategies for Efficient Filesystem Use

Partitioning is an essential aspect of filesystem management that directly influences system performance, scalability, and ease of management. The way storage devices are divided into logical sections—known as partitions—can have a significant impact on how efficiently the system uses available disk space, how quickly data can be accessed, and how easily the system can be maintained and expanded. Effective partitioning strategies allow system administrators to organize data in a way that optimizes performance, prevents data fragmentation, and simplifies backup and recovery processes. When done properly, partitioning ensures that disk space is used efficiently, helps isolate system components, and enhances security.

The first consideration in partitioning a disk is understanding the purpose of the system and the type of workload it will handle. Systems that serve as file servers, web servers, or databases may require different partitioning strategies than general-purpose systems or workstations. For example, a server running a database management system (DBMS) may benefit from dedicated partitions for the database files, logs, and backup data to ensure that each component has enough space and to optimize access times. Similarly, a system running a web server may benefit from separating the web server's root directory from its log files, as logs can grow rapidly and may require different management strategies than web content. By carefully considering the purpose and requirements of the system, administrators can tailor the partitioning scheme to meet the specific needs of the workload.

One of the most important partitioning strategies involves creating separate partitions for different components of the system. This approach helps to isolate critical system files from user data and application files. For instance, it is common to create separate partitions for the root filesystem (/), home directories (/home), and temporary files (/tmp). The root partition contains the core system files, libraries, and configurations, while the home partition is typically used for user data and personal files. The /tmp partition, on the other hand, is used for temporary files that may need to be cleared periodically. Separating these components allows administrators to allocate space based on the specific needs of each area. For example, the root partition may require a smaller allocation, while the home partition may need more space, depending on the number of users and the amount of data they generate.

Another key benefit of separating partitions is that it can improve system stability and performance. For example, if the /tmp directory fills up with temporary files, it will not affect the rest of the system, as it resides on its own partition. This isolation helps to prevent issues such as file system corruption or system slowdowns that could occur if the disk space on the root partition is exhausted. Additionally, partitioning allows for better disk space management by giving administrators more control over how space is allocated and preventing one part of the system from consuming all available disk space. For instance, if user data grows excessively, the home partition can be expanded without affecting the root filesystem or other components.

In environments where high performance is critical, partitioning can be used to optimize disk access times. For example, creating a separate partition for database files on a dedicated disk or a fast solid-state drive (SSD) can significantly improve database performance. Since database systems rely heavily on disk I/O, placing the database on a dedicated partition allows the system to access data more efficiently and reduces contention with other system processes. Similarly, placing log files on a separate partition or disk can help avoid performance degradation caused by excessive disk writes. The partitioning scheme should take into account the specific access patterns of the workload and the type of storage media being used to ensure that the system is optimized for speed and responsiveness.

For systems with multiple users, it is also beneficial to consider the creation of individual partitions or logical volumes for each user or group. This partitioning strategy helps to manage disk space on a per-user or per-group basis, ensuring that one user does not consume all available disk space at the expense of others. In multi-user environments, administrators can create user-specific partitions that restrict the amount of disk space available to each user. This is particularly important in shared environments where users may have different storage requirements. For instance, in a university or organization with many users, each user's home directory could be allocated a fixed amount of space, ensuring that one user's files do not impact others' ability to store their data.

Partitioning is also essential for system security. By separating sensitive system components, such as system configurations or data backups, into their own partitions, administrators can implement stronger access control mechanisms and ensure that sensitive data is protected from unauthorized access. For example, the /var partition, which is often used for logs, can be made read-only for non-administrative users, reducing the risk of tampering or unauthorized modifications. Similarly, partitioning can help with encryption by isolating specific volumes, such as a partition containing sensitive data, for encryption. This adds an additional layer of security, ensuring that if a physical disk is compromised or stolen, the encrypted data remains protected.

When it comes to expanding storage, partitioning plays a vital role in scalability. In systems where storage needs are expected to grow, partitioning allows administrators to scale storage resources without disrupting the entire system. Logical Volume Manager (LVM) is often used alongside partitioning to provide flexible and dynamic management of disk space. LVM allows for the creation of logical volumes that span across multiple physical disks, making it easier to add storage capacity as the system grows. This flexibility is particularly useful in virtualized environments, where virtual machines may require additional storage resources over time. LVM allows for the expansion of logical volumes without the need for downtime or reconfiguration, making it an ideal solution for systems with rapidly changing storage needs.

Another important consideration in partitioning is the alignment of partitions with the underlying storage media. When creating partitions on modern storage devices, such as SSDs or advanced format drives, ensuring proper alignment is crucial for optimal performance. Improper partition alignment can result in slower performance, as it can cause unnecessary read and write operations. Partition alignment tools are often used to ensure that partitions are correctly aligned with the storage device's internal block structure, thereby improving I/O performance and reducing wear on the storage media.

Managing partitions also involves monitoring their usage to prevent space exhaustion. Administrators should regularly check disk usage and ensure that partitions are not approaching their capacity. Tools like df and du are useful for monitoring disk usage and identifying areas where space is being consumed rapidly. When a partition is nearing full capacity, administrators can take proactive steps, such as extending the partition using tools like LVM or reorganizing data to optimize storage.

The process of partitioning is not only about creating physical divisions on a disk but also about creating a flexible, manageable, and scalable storage environment that can evolve as the system's needs change. By carefully considering the types of workloads, security needs, and future growth of the system, administrators can design a partitioning scheme that optimizes performance, ensures security, and facilitates scalability. Whether isolating system files from user data, improving performance through dedicated partitions, or managing disk space across multiple users, effective partitioning strategies are essential for maintaining an efficient and high-performing filesystem.

Filesystem Backups: Theory and Best Practices

Filesystem backups are one of the most critical aspects of data management, ensuring that valuable information is protected from unexpected events such as hardware failures, software corruption, or human error. A well-designed backup strategy can provide peace of mind, knowing that in the event of a disaster, critical data can be recovered, minimizing downtime and preventing data loss. The theory behind filesystem backups is straightforward—preserve a copy of important files and directories in case the primary data becomes inaccessible. However, the implementation of an effective backup strategy requires a deep understanding of different backup types, technologies, and best practices.

At the core of any backup strategy is the need to ensure data integrity and availability. When considering filesystem backups, it is important to first understand the concept of data redundancy. Redundancy involves creating duplicate copies of data and storing them in separate physical or cloud-based locations to ensure that a single point of failure does not result in complete data loss. This principle is crucial because a single hard drive failure, for example, could result in the loss of an entire system or application, including its data. Having multiple backup copies, both on-site and off-site, ensures that even in the case of a hardware disaster, there is always a recoverable version of the data.

There are several types of backups commonly used in filesystem management, each with its advantages and trade-offs. The most basic type is a full backup, which creates an exact copy of all the data in the filesystem. Full backups are comprehensive and easy to understand, but they can be time-consuming and require significant storage space. This makes them less practical for frequent backup schedules, especially when dealing with large filesystems or environments with limited storage resources. For this reason, many systems implement incremental or differential backups in combination with full backups.

Incremental backups only capture the changes made since the last backup, whether that be a full backup or the most recent incremental backup. This results in smaller backup files and reduces the time required to perform the backup process. However, restoring data from incremental backups can be more complicated and time-consuming, as it requires applying each incremental backup in sequence to recreate the full set of data. Differential backups, on the other hand, capture all the changes made since the last full backup. While they tend to be larger than incremental backups, restoring data from a differential backup is simpler, as only the full backup and the most recent differential backup need to be applied.

The choice between incremental and differential backups depends on the specific requirements of the environment. For instance, in environments where data changes frequently and storage space is limited, incremental backups may be more practical. However, in situations where fast recovery times are critical, differential backups may be preferred despite their larger size. Regardless of the approach, having a combination of full, incremental, and differential backups ensures that data can be restored in the most efficient way possible, depending on the situation.

Filesystem backups should not only be about data duplication but also about ensuring consistency. When backing up live systems, it is essential to ensure that the data being backed up is in a consistent state. This is especially true for databases or applications that may be in the middle of transactions when the backup is taken. Inconsistencies can lead to corruption in the backup, making it useless in a recovery scenario. To address this, many systems use techniques such as snapshotting, which captures the state of the filesystem at a specific point in time without interrupting active processes. For instance, many filesystems like ZFS and Btrfs provide built-in support for snapshots, which can be used to create a consistent backup without shutting down or pausing the system.

Once the data is backed up, the next challenge is storage. Backup storage can be classified into two main categories: on-site and off-site. On-site backups are stored within the same physical location as the original data, such as on a secondary hard drive or network-attached storage (NAS) device. On-site backups provide fast access for recovery and can be easier to manage, as they do not require internet connectivity or external services. However, they are vulnerable to the same risks as the primary data—such as fire, theft, or flood—so relying solely on on-site backups exposes the system to significant risk.

Off-site backups, on the other hand, are stored in a separate physical location, either in a remote data center or in the cloud. Off-site backups protect against local disasters and ensure that data is available even in catastrophic scenarios. Cloud-based storage solutions, such as Amazon Web Services (AWS), Google Cloud, and Microsoft Azure, offer scalable and secure storage options for backups. Cloud backups can be automated, encrypted, and geographically dispersed, which reduces the risk of data loss due to hardware failure, natural disasters, or other localized issues. One challenge with off-site backups is that recovery times may be longer compared to on-site backups, particularly when dealing with large datasets. However, many modern cloud providers offer features like fast recovery times, deduplication, and versioning, which help mitigate these challenges.

One of the most critical aspects of filesystem backups is automation. A manual backup process is not only time-consuming but also prone to human error, making it an unreliable solution for critical systems. Automating backups ensures that data is backed up regularly and without fail, reducing the risk of missing scheduled backups. Most modern systems include built-in backup tools or third-party solutions that allow for easy automation of backup tasks. For instance, cron jobs in Linux can be used to schedule regular backups at specific intervals, while backup software like Veeam or Acronis can manage backups on a larger scale, including remote or cloud-based backups. Automated backups should be tested regularly to ensure they are functioning as expected and that data can be recovered when needed.

Regularly testing the integrity of backups is another key practice in maintaining a reliable backup strategy. Even the best backup systems can fail if the data being backed up is corrupted or incomplete. Regularly performing test restores ensures that backup copies are intact and usable in the event of a disaster. These tests help identify any issues in the backup process, such as incomplete backups, incorrect configurations, or storage failures, before they can affect production systems.

Another important consideration is encryption. Filesystem backups often contain sensitive or confidential information, making it critical to protect backup data both in transit and at rest. Many backup solutions support encryption, which ensures that even if a backup is intercepted or compromised, the data remains unreadable without the appropriate decryption key. Ensuring that backups are encrypted, particularly for off-site storage, adds an essential layer of security, especially when using cloud-based storage providers.

In large-scale environments, backup strategies should also include versioning, which allows administrators to retain multiple versions of the same file or dataset over time. Versioning ensures that if a file becomes corrupted or deleted, a previous, unaltered version can be restored. This practice is especially important for databases or systems that generate large amounts of data, as it allows administrators to roll back to a previous state without losing large amounts of information.

Filesystem backups are a fundamental aspect of maintaining data integrity and availability. A well-planned and well-executed backup strategy protects against data loss, ensures business continuity, and provides peace of mind. By understanding the different types of backups, selecting the right storage solution, automating the backup process, and regularly testing and securing backups, system administrators can safeguard their systems against the unexpected and ensure that data remains accessible and secure in the face of disaster.

Backup Types: Full, Incremental, and Differential

Backups are essential for protecting data from loss due to accidental deletion, hardware failure, corruption, or disasters. The choice of backup type plays a crucial role in shaping the efficiency and effectiveness of the backup strategy. Among the most commonly used backup types are full, incremental, and differential backups. Each type has its own benefits and drawbacks, and understanding these differences helps system administrators design a backup system that meets the specific needs of their environment, ensuring that data can be restored quickly and reliably in case of an emergency.

A full backup is the most comprehensive and straightforward type of backup. It involves making an exact copy of all the data, including system files, applications, and user data, on the target system. This backup captures everything, regardless of whether the data has changed since the last backup or not. The main advantage of a full backup is its simplicity and ease of use. Since the backup is a complete copy of the entire filesystem, restoring data is straightforward and fast. In the event of a disaster, the system can be fully restored to its previous state using just one backup.

However, while full backups are simple and reliable, they come with some significant drawbacks, primarily related to storage requirements and time. Full backups can be large in size, particularly for systems with large amounts of data. This means that they require substantial storage space, and the process of creating the backup can be time-consuming. For systems with frequent changes in data or large datasets, performing full backups regularly can quickly become impractical. Given these limitations, full backups are typically performed on a periodic basis, often weekly or monthly, with other types of backups used more frequently in between.

To mitigate the storage and time costs of full backups, incremental backups are often used. An incremental backup only captures the changes made since the last backup, whether that was a full or an incremental backup. This means that instead of copying all the data, the backup process is faster and requires less storage, as only new or modified data is included. For instance, if a full backup is taken on Sunday and incremental backups are taken on Monday, Tuesday, and Wednesday, the backup on Monday will only include changes made since Sunday, and the backup on Tuesday will only include changes made since Monday.

The primary advantage of incremental backups is their efficiency in terms of storage space and time. Since they only store the data that has changed since the last backup, they are much smaller and faster to create than full backups. This makes incremental backups particularly useful for systems with large amounts of data or systems that require frequent backups, such as databases or web servers. In environments where time and storage are limited, incremental backups can significantly reduce the impact on system performance and storage resources.

However, while incremental backups are efficient, they come with their own set of challenges. One major drawback is the complexity of the restore process. To fully restore a system from incremental backups, not just the most recent incremental backup but all previous backups from the point of the full backup onward must be applied in sequence. This means that if one of the incremental backups is corrupted or lost, the entire restore process may fail, and the data may not be recoverable. Additionally, restoring from incremental backups can take longer than restoring from a full backup, as the system must go through each incremental backup in order.

Differential backups offer a middle ground between full and incremental backups. A differential backup captures all the changes made since the last full backup, regardless of the number of intermediate incremental backups. This means that while a differential backup is larger than an incremental backup, it is still smaller than a full backup. The key difference between differential and incremental backups lies in how the changes are recorded. Unlike incremental backups, which only store changes since the last backup (whether full or incremental), differential backups include all changes made since the most recent full backup.

The advantage of differential backups is that they simplify the restore process. To restore from a differential backup, only the last full backup and the most recent differential backup are required. This eliminates the need to apply a chain of incremental backups, as is necessary with incremental backups. As a result, differential backups offer faster restore times compared to incremental backups. However, as more time passes since the last full backup, the size of the differential backup increases, as it includes all changes made during that time. This means that over time, differential backups can become nearly as large as a full backup, particularly in environments with significant changes in data.

Differential backups are useful in situations where a balance between storage efficiency and restore time is needed. They provide faster restores than incremental backups while still offering some level of storage efficiency. However, since the size of differential backups increases over time, they may not be as storage-efficient as incremental backups, especially in environments with a high rate of data changes. Differential backups are often used in conjunction with full backups and incremental backups in a hybrid backup strategy, providing a balance between storage usage and restore speed.

One of the primary challenges with all types of backups is ensuring that the backup strategy is tailored to the specific needs of the environment. For example, for systems where data is constantly changing, such as web servers or database systems, a combination of full, incremental, and differential backups may be necessary to strike the right balance between speed, storage efficiency, and restore time. A common approach is to take a full backup on a weekly or monthly basis and use incremental backups daily to capture changes between full backups. Differential backups can then be used as needed, typically on a less frequent basis, to ensure fast recovery in the event of data loss.

Another important consideration is backup frequency. For mission-critical systems where data loss cannot be tolerated, backups should be performed frequently, and a combination of full, incremental, and differential backups can help ensure that data is consistently protected. In environments where data changes infrequently, or where data loss is less critical, less frequent backups may be sufficient, and the strategy may lean more heavily on full backups with occasional differential backups.

Data integrity is also a key factor in backup strategy. Backup systems must ensure that the data being backed up is accurate and consistent. This is particularly important for systems running databases or transactional systems, where a partial backup or a corrupted backup could result in data corruption or inconsistencies upon restore. Techniques such as snapshotting or using backup solutions that support consistency checks are essential for ensuring that backups are reliable.

Selecting the right combination of full, incremental, and differential backups is essential for creating a reliable and efficient backup system. Each backup type has its strengths and weaknesses, and understanding these differences allows system administrators to design a backup strategy that meets the specific needs of their systems. By combining these strategies effectively, administrators can ensure that data is backed up regularly, efficiently, and can be restored quickly when needed.

Designing a Backup Strategy for SysAdmins

Designing an effective backup strategy is one of the most crucial responsibilities for system administrators (sysadmins), as it ensures the integrity, availability, and recoverability of critical data. A backup strategy involves more than just creating copies of files; it is about creating a comprehensive and reliable process that can restore the system to a functional state in the event of hardware failure, accidental data deletion, software corruption, or even natural disasters. A solid backup plan not only safeguards data but also provides peace of mind, knowing that there is a reliable mechanism to recover from unexpected events.

The first step in designing a backup strategy is to understand the specific needs of the environment, including the types of data being protected, the criticality of that data, and the acceptable downtime in the event of a failure. Not all data is equally important, and different systems and services may have different recovery objectives. For example, in a business-critical environment, a database system may need near-instant recovery, while less critical data, such as archived logs, may not require the same level of attention. Understanding these factors allows sysadmins to prioritize backup tasks and allocate resources where they are needed most.

Once the criticality of the data is assessed, the next consideration is the frequency of backups. The frequency of backups largely depends on how often the data changes. For systems that handle transactional or real-time data, such as databases, frequent backups are essential to ensure that the latest changes are protected. In contrast, systems that store static data may only need periodic backups. Sysadmins must strike a balance between backup frequency, storage requirements, and system performance. More frequent backups increase storage consumption and may slow down system performance during the backup process, but they provide a higher level of protection. Less frequent backups, on the other hand, may save storage space and reduce system load but can result in greater data loss in case of a failure.

The type of backup also plays a significant role in designing an effective backup strategy. Full backups, incremental backups, and differential backups each have their advantages and disadvantages, and understanding these differences is key to balancing efficiency and reliability. Full backups create complete copies of the entire dataset, making them easy to restore but requiring more storage space and longer backup times. Incremental backups only store changes since the last backup, making them more efficient in terms of storage but more complex when it comes to restoration, as all incremental backups since the last full backup must be applied in sequence. Differential backups, which capture all changes made since the last full backup, offer a middle ground by providing faster restores than incremental backups, though they may require more storage as time passes.

A hybrid approach often works best, combining full, incremental, and differential backups to create a strategy that is both efficient and resilient. For example, sysadmins may schedule full backups on a weekly basis while taking incremental backups daily. Differential backups can be used as an additional safety measure or on a less frequent basis to ensure that restores are more straightforward. By using this combination, sysadmins can ensure that backup copies are both manageable in size and easy to restore in case of a disaster.

Another critical component of a backup strategy is the choice of backup storage. The location of backups must be carefully considered to ensure that they are both secure and accessible when needed. On-site backups, stored on local storage devices or network-attached storage (NAS), offer fast recovery times and are easy to manage. However, on-site backups are vulnerable to local disasters such as fire, flooding, or theft. To mitigate these risks, off-site backups should be part of the strategy. Off-site backups, stored in remote data centers or cloud environments, provide an additional layer of protection by ensuring that data is safe even if the primary site is compromised. Cloud storage is increasingly popular due to its scalability, flexibility, and accessibility, allowing backups to be automated and managed without requiring physical hardware.

Encrypting backups is another important best practice in a backup strategy. Data encryption ensures that even if backup files are compromised, the information remains unreadable without the appropriate decryption key. Sysadmins should ensure that both on-site and off-site backups are encrypted, particularly when using cloud-based storage services, as the data may traverse the internet or be stored on shared infrastructure. Strong encryption standards, such as AES-256, should be used to ensure that backup data remains secure during transit and at rest. Additionally, encryption adds an extra layer of protection against unauthorized access, helping to safeguard sensitive or confidential information.

Retention policies also need to be carefully considered when designing a backup strategy. Retention policies define how long backup data should be kept before it is deleted or archived. Retaining backups for too long can result in unnecessary storage usage, while retaining them for too short a period can leave systems vulnerable to data loss. A good retention policy balances the need for data availability with storage efficiency. Retention can be tiered based on the importance of the data, with more recent backups kept for longer periods and older backups archived or deleted once they are no longer deemed useful. For example, full backups could be kept for a month, while incremental backups may be deleted after a week, and archived backups could be stored for a year or longer, depending on regulatory or organizational requirements.

Automating the backup process is another key aspect of a reliable backup strategy. Manual backups are prone to human error and can be inconsistent, which increases the risk of data loss. By automating backup tasks, sysadmins can ensure that backups are performed on time and that the data is protected without requiring constant oversight. Most modern backup solutions, both software and hardware-based, offer features such as scheduled backups, backup verification, and reporting tools to automate the backup process. These features not only reduce the administrative burden but also help ensure that backups are consistent and reliable.

Monitoring and testing backups is an often-overlooked part of the backup process but is essential to ensure that backup data is both recoverable and complete. Backup logs should be reviewed regularly to ensure that no errors occurred during the backup process, and sysadmins should periodically perform test restores to verify that backup files are intact and usable. Regular testing can help identify potential issues before they affect the system, such as corrupt backups or missing files, ensuring that the recovery process will be smooth and efficient when needed.

Finally, documenting the backup strategy and recovery procedures is essential for ensuring that backup and recovery operations are carried out effectively. A well-documented plan includes details about the backup schedule, storage locations, retention policies, encryption methods, and recovery procedures. This documentation should be easily accessible and regularly updated to reflect any changes in the system or backup strategy. Furthermore, having a clear recovery plan ensures that sysadmins can act quickly and efficiently during a disaster, reducing downtime and minimizing the impact on the organization.

Designing a robust backup strategy is a multifaceted task that requires careful planning and consideration. By evaluating the specific needs of the environment, selecting appropriate backup types, ensuring data redundancy, and implementing best practices for backup storage, encryption, retention, and testing, sysadmins can create a reliable backup system that safeguards critical data and ensures business continuity. A well-designed backup strategy is not just about creating copies of data; it is about creating a comprehensive safety net that ensures data availability and minimizes risk in the event of a system failure or disaster.

Understanding Backup Schedules and Retention Policies

Backup schedules and retention policies are fundamental components of a robust data protection strategy. Without a well-planned backup schedule, critical data may not be protected in a timely manner, leaving systems vulnerable to data loss. Similarly, retention policies play an essential role in managing the lifecycle of backup data, ensuring that old and unnecessary backups are cleared to make room for new ones while still retaining essential data for recovery needs. Understanding how to design and implement both backup schedules and retention policies is critical for system administrators to strike the right balance between data protection, storage efficiency, and compliance requirements.

A backup schedule defines when and how often backups will occur. The goal is to create a schedule that ensures data is consistently protected without overburdening system resources or storage capacity. The first step in creating an effective backup schedule is to assess the frequency at which data changes. For example, in environments where data is frequently modified or added, such as transactional systems or databases, more frequent backups are required to ensure that recent changes are protected. On the other hand, in systems with static data, backups can be performed less frequently. The schedule should align with the system's data volatility and its recovery objectives. Backup schedules can vary widely based on the size of the organization, the type of data, and the systems involved.

The most common types of backup schedules are daily, weekly, and monthly. A daily backup schedule might include incremental backups, which only capture changes made since the last backup, making them faster and less storage-intensive. Incremental backups can be scheduled at night when system usage is low, reducing the impact on system performance. Weekly backups, often full backups, create a complete copy of the data and are typically scheduled during off-peak hours. Full backups provide a reliable point-in-time copy of the data, which is important for ensuring that all data is captured accurately and fully. Monthly backups may also be included in the schedule, serving as a long-term retention point and often stored in an off-site location to protect against data loss due to physical damage to the primary site.

One of the challenges in creating a backup schedule is ensuring that backups do not disrupt system performance or availability. Running large backups during business hours, for example, can cause significant slowdowns, making it difficult for users to access the system. To minimize this impact, backups should be carefully scheduled to occur during periods of low system usage, such as overnight or during weekends. For high-demand environments, where downtime is unacceptable, administrators may need to use backup solutions that allow for live backups or snapshots. These methods enable backups to be taken without interrupting active users or services, ensuring that critical applications remain available while the backup is being performed.

Once the backup schedule is in place, retention policies need to be defined to determine how long backup data is kept. Retention policies govern the lifecycle of backup data, specifying how long different types of backups are retained and when they should be deleted or archived. Retention policies are important for managing storage space, ensuring compliance with legal or regulatory requirements, and maintaining an organized backup system. Without a clear retention policy, backups can accumulate rapidly, consuming valuable storage resources and leading to inefficiencies in backup management. Moreover, excessive retention of unnecessary backups can create confusion during the recovery process, making it more difficult to locate the right version of the data when needed.

The retention policy should be based on the organization's data recovery needs, legal and regulatory requirements, and storage capacity. Different types of backups may have different retention periods depending on their importance. For example, full backups might be retained for a longer period, such as several months or even years, while incremental backups may only need to be kept for a few days or weeks. In some industries, such as healthcare or finance, there may be specific compliance requirements dictating the minimum retention period for certain types of data. For instance, financial records might need to be stored for a specific number of years, while less critical data could be deleted after a shorter period. Retention policies help organizations comply with these legal obligations by ensuring that backups are kept for the required duration.

Retention policies should also take into account the frequency of data changes. For data that is frequently updated or overwritten, shorter retention periods may be sufficient, as recent backups will already contain the latest information. On the other hand, systems with infrequent changes or where historical data is valuable may require longer retention periods. For example, a database system used for transactional processing might have daily incremental backups, but full backups might be retained for a longer period to ensure that the entire database can be restored in case of a disaster. Archiving older backups that are no longer required for daily operations can be an effective way to manage space while still retaining the data for future use.

Storage efficiency is another key consideration when setting retention policies. Backups consume storage space, and without proper management, this space can quickly become a bottleneck. One common approach to improving storage efficiency is to implement deduplication, a process that eliminates duplicate copies of data across backups. Deduplication ensures that only unique data is stored, helping to reduce storage requirements while maintaining the integrity of the backups. Additionally, backups can be compressed to further save storage space. By retaining only the most recent full backups and a minimal set of incremental or differential backups, administrators can significantly reduce the amount of storage required for long-term data retention.

In environments where off-site or cloud storage is used for backups, managing retention becomes even more important. Storing backups in the cloud can be cost-effective, but long retention periods can lead to high storage costs. Many cloud storage providers offer tiered pricing models, where frequently accessed data is more expensive to store, while infrequently accessed data can be stored at a lower cost. Administrators can take advantage of these pricing models by creating retention policies that archive older backups to less expensive storage tiers, ensuring that the system remains cost-effective without compromising data protection. In such setups, backup data might be moved to cold storage or archived after a certain retention period, further optimizing storage resources.

In addition to managing the data itself, it is important for sysadmins to regularly review and update backup schedules and retention policies. As systems evolve and data usage patterns change, backup strategies should be adjusted to ensure they continue to meet the organization's needs. Regular testing and verification of backups are also essential, as they help ensure that the data can be restored successfully when needed. Backups should be monitored to detect any failures, and the system should generate reports to alert administrators to issues in the backup process.

Ultimately, backup schedules and retention policies are vital to ensuring that backup data is managed efficiently, securely, and in a way that aligns with the organization's operational and regulatory requirements. By carefully designing backup schedules that account for data change frequency, system performance, and business needs, sysadmins can ensure that critical data is regularly protected without disrupting system performance. Equally, by implementing thoughtful retention policies that balance storage efficiency, legal requirements, and the need for historical data, organizations can optimize their backup storage while ensuring compliance and long-term data availability.

Network-Based Backup Solutions

Network-based backup solutions play a vital role in modern data protection strategies, providing organizations with the ability to safeguard critical data efficiently and securely across multiple devices and locations. Unlike traditional local backup methods, network-based backups enable the storage of backup data on remote systems or network-attached storage (NAS), offering flexibility, scalability, and enhanced security. These solutions are increasingly essential in environments where data is spread across various servers, workstations, and remote offices, providing an effective means of centralizing data protection efforts while minimizing physical storage requirements.

One of the key advantages of network-based backup solutions is their ability to centralize backups in a single location, making it easier to manage and monitor the backup process. Rather than relying on local backups, which may be scattered across individual machines or storage devices, network-based solutions consolidate backup data into a central repository. This centralization simplifies backup management, as administrators can monitor the status of all backups, schedule tasks, and verify the integrity of backup files from a single interface. By doing so, network-based backup solutions provide greater visibility and control over the backup process, reducing the risk of errors and ensuring that critical data is consistently protected.

Another significant benefit of network-based backups is their ability to scale with growing data requirements. As organizations expand, so do their storage needs. Network-based backup solutions can easily accommodate this growth by adding more storage devices to the network or expanding existing storage systems. For example, adding additional NAS devices or expanding cloud storage capacity can ensure that backups can continue uninterrupted as data volumes increase. This scalability is particularly beneficial in cloud-based environments, where storage resources can be dynamically allocated and managed without the need for significant upfront investment in physical hardware. As a result, network-based backup solutions provide a flexible and cost-effective means of protecting data in environments with evolving storage needs.

Security is another crucial aspect of network-based backup solutions. Data protection must not only focus on ensuring that backups are available but also on ensuring that the backup data is secure. Network-based solutions typically offer advanced security features such as encryption, both during transmission and at rest. When backing up data over a network, especially when using cloud storage, the data is often transmitted over the internet, which can expose it to potential threats. Encryption ensures that the data remains unreadable to unauthorized parties, safeguarding it from cyber-attacks or data breaches. Many network-based backup solutions also include secure authentication mechanisms, such as multi-factor authentication (MFA), which further enhance the security of the backup process by ensuring that only authorized users can access or modify backup data.

Network-based backup solutions also provide enhanced data redundancy and reliability. By storing backup copies in multiple locations, such as in remote data centers or across geographically distributed NAS devices, these solutions ensure that data is protected even in the event of a localized disaster. For example, if a fire or flood damages the primary office, the backup data stored in a remote location remains safe and can be quickly restored to resume normal business operations. Many solutions also integrate with technologies like RAID (Redundant Array of Independent Disks), which provides additional fault tolerance by mirroring or striping data across multiple disks. This redundancy is especially important for mission-critical data that must be available at all times, such as financial records or customer databases.

A key feature of network-based backup solutions is the ability to automate backup processes, reducing the need for manual intervention and minimizing the risk of human error. Scheduled backups can be configured to run at regular intervals, ensuring that data is consistently backed up without requiring constant oversight. Automated backup solutions can be customized to fit the organization's specific needs, whether performing daily incremental backups, weekly full backups, or continuous backups for real-time data protection. Automation also ensures that backups occur during off-peak hours, reducing the impact on system performance during business hours. This not only improves operational efficiency but also ensures that the backup process is predictable and reliable.

While network-based backups offer many advantages, there are also challenges that must be addressed to maximize their effectiveness. One of the primary challenges is network bandwidth. Backing up large amounts of data over a network, especially when using cloud-based solutions, can consume significant bandwidth and impact other critical network functions. To mitigate this, many network-based backup solutions employ techniques such as data deduplication, which eliminates redundant copies of data before transmission, reducing the amount of data that needs to be transferred. Additionally, some solutions offer features like bandwidth throttling, which allows administrators to control the amount of network bandwidth allocated to the backup process, ensuring that backups do not disrupt other network operations.

Another challenge of network-based backups is ensuring that backup data can be restored quickly and reliably when needed. While backups are essential for data protection, the true value of a backup system lies in its ability to restore data efficiently in the event of a failure. Network-based backup solutions must be designed to support fast and reliable restores, particularly for large datasets. Many solutions offer features like block-level restore, which allows for the restoration of only the modified portions of files, speeding up the recovery process. Additionally, cloud-based backup solutions often allow for flexible recovery options, such as the ability to restore data to different locations or virtual machines, which can be critical for businesses with complex infrastructures or disaster recovery needs.

The choice of network-based backup solution depends on several factors, including the size of the organization, the volume of data to be backed up, and the specific recovery requirements. Small to medium-sized businesses (SMBs) often benefit from affordable cloud-based backup solutions that offer scalability and off-site protection without the need for significant infrastructure investments. These solutions are easy to manage and provide a cost-effective means of backing up critical data. Larger organizations, on the other hand, may require more robust solutions that can handle large volumes of data, provide granular control over backup processes, and support advanced features such as continuous data protection and disaster recovery.

Ultimately, network-based backup solutions are essential for organizations looking to secure their data and ensure business continuity. By leveraging the flexibility, scalability, and security of network-based solutions, organizations can protect their data from loss and disaster, streamline backup management, and simplify the recovery process. While there are challenges to overcome, such as network bandwidth limitations and the need for reliable restore options, the benefits of network-based backup solutions far outweigh these challenges, making them an indispensable part of any modern data protection strategy.

Cloud Storage for Backup Solutions

Cloud storage has revolutionized the way businesses and individuals handle data backup by offering an off-site, scalable, and highly available solution for safeguarding data. The traditional methods of backing up data, such as using external hard drives or on-premises storage devices, have their limitations, including physical space constraints, vulnerability to disasters, and higher management costs. Cloud storage addresses these issues by providing a more flexible, cost-effective, and secure alternative. As data continues to grow at an unprecedented rate, especially with the proliferation of digital content and the increasing reliance on cloud-based services, cloud storage for backup solutions has become an essential tool for modern data protection strategies.

Cloud storage offers numerous advantages for backup solutions, the most significant being its scalability. With traditional on-premises backup solutions, businesses are often limited by the physical storage space available on their servers or external devices. As data grows, organizations are required to continually invest in additional storage infrastructure to keep up with their expanding needs. In contrast, cloud storage allows businesses to scale their storage needs up or down based on actual demand. This on-demand scalability is particularly valuable for organizations experiencing rapid data growth or those with fluctuating storage needs. Cloud providers offer various storage tiers, from low-cost, infrequent access storage to high-performance solutions, giving businesses the flexibility to choose the right option for their backup requirements.

The cost-effectiveness of cloud storage is another compelling reason for its widespread adoption in backup solutions. Traditional backup methods often require significant capital expenditures for physical storage devices, data centers, and backup software. These systems also require ongoing maintenance and personnel resources to ensure they operate efficiently. Cloud storage, on the other hand, typically operates on a pay-as-you-go model, meaning businesses only pay for the storage they use. This significantly reduces upfront costs and allows organizations to better manage their storage expenses over time. Furthermore, the cloud eliminates the need for maintaining physical infrastructure, reducing operational overheads such as power consumption, cooling, and equipment upkeep.

Another important benefit of cloud storage for backup solutions is its inherent data redundancy and availability. Cloud providers typically replicate data across multiple geographic locations, ensuring that backups are safe from localized disasters, such as fires, floods, or thefts. This level of redundancy is difficult and expensive to achieve with on-premises backup solutions. If an organization's data is stored in multiple data centers, it can be restored quickly even if one location is compromised. This high availability and disaster recovery capability make cloud storage an ideal solution for businesses that cannot afford downtime or data loss. Cloud providers often guarantee certain levels of service uptime through service level agreements (SLAs), ensuring that businesses can rely on their backup solution to maintain availability and business continuity.

Security is one of the key concerns when it comes to data storage, and cloud providers have invested heavily in securing their storage environments. Most reputable cloud storage providers implement robust encryption protocols to protect data both during transit and while stored at rest. Data encryption ensures that even if a malicious actor gains access to the data, they will be unable to read it without the appropriate decryption keys. Cloud providers also offer various authentication mechanisms, including multi-factor authentication (MFA), to protect access to backup data. Moreover, many cloud storage services provide granular access controls, allowing organizations to define who can access or modify backup data. These security measures make cloud storage a secure and compliant solution for backing up sensitive or regulated data, such as personal information, financial records, or healthcare data.

One of the most attractive features of cloud storage for backup solutions is its ease of use. Cloud storage systems typically offer user-friendly interfaces and automation features that make managing backups more efficient. Many cloud storage providers offer integrated backup software that automates the entire backup process, including scheduling, monitoring, and notifications. With cloud backup solutions, businesses can set up automatic backup schedules that run without manual intervention, reducing the chances of human error and ensuring that backups occur regularly. These automation features are particularly valuable in large-scale environments with multiple servers or endpoints, where manually managing backups would be impractical.

Furthermore, cloud storage enables centralized backup management. In the past, businesses often needed to manage multiple physical backup devices spread across different locations, making it difficult to ensure consistency and track backup status. With cloud storage, all backup data can be centralized in a single, remote location, making it easier to monitor the health of backups, perform restorations, and audit backup activities. This centralization of backup data not only streamlines management but also provides greater visibility and control over the backup process, which is critical for organizations looking to improve their data protection strategies.

Cloud storage for backup solutions also supports the concept of versioning, allowing businesses to retain multiple versions of their data over time. This is particularly important in environments where data changes frequently, such as in collaborative workspaces or content management systems. Versioning enables businesses to recover previous iterations of files or databases, providing protection against accidental overwrites, deletions, or corruption. In the event of a ransomware attack or other forms of data corruption, businesses can quickly revert to an uninfected backup version, reducing the impact of the attack.

However, despite the many benefits of cloud storage for backup solutions, there are some considerations and challenges that organizations must address when implementing cloud-based backups. One of the primary challenges is the potential for bandwidth limitations. Backing up large volumes of data to the cloud can be time-consuming and costly, particularly for organizations with limited internet bandwidth or high volumes of data to transfer. The initial backup process can be slow, as it often involves uploading large datasets to the cloud. Some cloud providers address this challenge by offering features like bandwidth throttling, which allows businesses to manage how much bandwidth is allocated to the backup process, ensuring that it does not interfere with other critical network activities. Additionally, many cloud providers offer data seeding options, where businesses can send physical copies of their data to the provider for initial upload, which can speed up the process.

Data recovery times can also be a concern with cloud-based backup solutions, especially when dealing with large datasets. While cloud storage provides excellent redundancy and availability, the speed of data recovery can be impacted by factors such as internet speed and the amount of data to be restored. For businesses that require fast recovery times, cloud providers often offer additional options, such as expedited recovery or the ability to restore data to virtual machines, to speed up the restoration process.

The ongoing costs of cloud storage should also be considered when implementing a cloud backup solution. While cloud storage eliminates the need for significant capital expenditures on hardware, organizations must manage the ongoing costs of storing data in the cloud. The pay-as-you-go model can be highly cost-effective for businesses with fluctuating storage needs, but organizations need to carefully monitor usage to ensure they are not overpaying for unused or unnecessary storage. Most cloud providers offer cost calculators and usage reports to help organizations optimize their storage expenditures.

Cloud storage for backup solutions has become an essential tool for modern data protection. By offering scalability, flexibility, security, and ease of use, cloud storage allows businesses to implement reliable and cost-effective backup strategies that protect their data from loss, corruption, or disaster. While challenges such as bandwidth limitations and recovery times should be taken into account, the benefits of cloud storage far outweigh the drawbacks, making it an indispensable component of any comprehensive data protection plan.

Using rsync for Backup Automation

Rsync is a powerful tool commonly used in Linux and Unix-like systems for synchronizing files and directories between two locations. While its original purpose was to copy files from one system to another, it has evolved into a versatile solution for creating and automating backups. Using rsync for backup automation offers several advantages, including speed, flexibility, and efficiency. It allows administrators to set up backup schedules, automate file transfers, and ensure that backup operations run with minimal human intervention. By understanding how rsync works and how to configure it for backup automation, system administrators can design efficient, reliable, and secure backup solutions for their systems.

At its core, rsync is a file synchronization tool that copies only the changes made to files, rather than duplicating the entire file set each time. This is accomplished using a delta-transfer algorithm, which identifies differences between the source and destination files and only transfers the parts that have been modified. This makes rsync highly efficient in terms of bandwidth and storage usage. When used for backup automation, rsync ensures that only new or modified files are copied to the backup location, which reduces the amount of time required for backup tasks and minimizes storage requirements. Additionally, rsync can be used to back up data over a network, allowing for remote backups that are both secure and fast.

One of the primary benefits of using rsync for backup automation is its ability to handle incremental backups. With incremental backups, only the files that have changed since the last backup are copied. This minimizes the amount of data transferred and stored, making backups faster and more efficient. In a typical backup scenario, an initial full backup might be taken to establish a baseline. After that, subsequent backups only copy the changes that have occurred since the previous backup, whether it's a full or incremental one. Rsync excels at this task, allowing system administrators to easily create an incremental backup system that runs regularly without requiring excessive resources.

Rsync can be used to automate backups by creating simple scripts that execute on a scheduled basis. These scripts can be set to run at specific intervals, such as daily, weekly, or monthly, depending on the organization's needs. To accomplish this, administrators can use cron jobs, which are a standard way of scheduling tasks on Linux systems. Cron allows for precise scheduling, so a backup script can be set to run during off-peak hours, reducing the load on the system during business hours. By automating the backup process, administrators can ensure that backups occur consistently without the need for manual intervention. This not only saves time but also reduces the risk of human error.

Another useful feature of rsync for backup automation is its ability to synchronize files across different machines. By using rsync over SSH (Secure Shell), administrators can securely back up data from remote systems. This is particularly useful in distributed environments where data is stored on multiple servers or across various locations. Rsync over SSH encrypts the data during transit, ensuring that sensitive information remains protected. By configuring rsync to run automatically on a schedule, system administrators can set up a remote backup system that is both secure and efficient. Whether backing up data to a central server or to cloud storage, rsync can be customized to meet the needs of diverse backup scenarios.

Rsync also supports various options for handling file permissions, timestamps, and symbolic links. This ensures that the backup copy maintains the same file attributes as the source files. For example, the -a (archive) option in rsync preserves file permissions, symbolic links, and timestamps, ensuring that the backup is an exact replica of the original data. This is particularly important in situations where file integrity and metadata need to be preserved. Additionally, rsync can be configured to delete files from the backup location if they are removed from the source, ensuring that the backup remains up to date. This makes rsync ideal for maintaining mirror backups, where the backup is meant to be an exact copy of the source data.

For administrators looking for more advanced backup solutions, rsync can also be used in conjunction with other tools and technologies to enhance its functionality. For instance, when backing up large amounts of data, rsync can be paired with compression tools to reduce the size of the backup files. Using the -z (compress) option in rsync can help minimize the amount of bandwidth required for remote backups, making it more efficient for backing up large datasets over slower network connections. In environments where backup data needs to be encrypted, rsync can be used with encryption tools like GPG or OpenSSL to ensure that sensitive data is securely stored during the backup process.

One potential drawback of rsync for backup automation is its lack of built-in features for managing complex backup schedules or storing multiple backup versions. Unlike some commercial backup solutions, rsync does not have a graphical interface or a sophisticated backup management system that tracks backup versions or retention policies. However, this limitation can be addressed through the use of custom scripts. For example, administrators can create scripts that rotate backup files, keeping multiple versions of the backup over time and deleting older backups according to a defined retention policy. By incorporating file versioning and retention logic into the backup scripts, administrators can overcome this limitation and create a more robust backup system.

Rsync also requires administrators to manage the backup storage locations, including monitoring disk space usage and ensuring that backups do not run out of storage. While rsync is efficient in terms of bandwidth and storage usage, it is still essential to monitor the backup destination and ensure that there is enough space for new backups. In cases where the backup destination is a local disk, administrators must also ensure that the disk is regularly maintained, as failures in the storage system could result in lost backup data. Using cloud storage for backup can alleviate some of these concerns, as cloud providers typically offer scalable storage options and ensure that the backup destination is always available. However, even in cloud-based backups, monitoring storage usage and managing retention policies is essential to ensure that costs do not spiral out of control.

One of the key aspects of using rsync for backup automation is its flexibility. Rsync can be configured to perform a variety of backup tasks, such as creating backups of specific directories, excluding certain files, and controlling the level of detail included in the backups. Administrators can fine-tune the backup process to meet the unique needs of their systems, whether they are backing up a few files or an entire file system. The flexibility of rsync also allows it to be used in a wide range of environments, from small home setups to large enterprise systems, making it a versatile and invaluable tool for system administrators.

Using rsync for backup automation is an efficient and cost-effective way to protect important data, especially in environments where flexibility, security, and performance are critical. Its ability to perform incremental backups, synchronize files over networks, and be easily automated makes it an ideal solution for managing backups in diverse environments. While it requires some setup and scripting knowledge, the benefits of rsync far outweigh the complexities, especially when compared to traditional backup methods. By leveraging the full capabilities of rsync, sysadmins can build a highly effective backup system that ensures data is safely stored and easily recoverable when needed.

Backup Encryption and Security Considerations

In an era of increasing cyber threats and data breaches, securing backup data has become a critical aspect of an organization's overall data protection strategy. Backup encryption and security considerations ensure that backup copies of important files, databases, and system configurations are protected not only from accidental loss but also from unauthorized access. While backups are essential for recovery in the event of data corruption, system failure, or cyberattacks, they can also become prime targets for attackers if left unprotected. If backup data is compromised, it could lead to data theft, ransomware attacks, or complete system compromise. Therefore, understanding the importance of backup encryption and the security measures needed to protect backup systems is crucial for organizations looking to safeguard their critical data assets.

Backup encryption involves the process of transforming backup data into a format that can only be read or accessed by authorized individuals. This is achieved using encryption algorithms that render the data unreadable to anyone without the decryption key or credentials. When sensitive information is encrypted during the backup process, it ensures that even if an attacker gains access to the backup media, the data remains unreadable and secure. Encryption plays a vital role in protecting both on-site and off-site backups, particularly in cloud storage solutions where data is transmitted over the internet. Without encryption, data could potentially be intercepted during transmission or accessed by malicious actors once it is stored in remote servers.

The need for encryption is particularly significant in industries handling sensitive or regulated data, such as healthcare, finance, and government sectors. These industries are subject to strict compliance regulations, such as HIPAA, PCI-DSS, and GDPR, which mandate that sensitive data, including backup data, be encrypted to protect the privacy of individuals and ensure data integrity. For example, in healthcare, patient records must be protected by encryption to prevent unauthorized access or theft, and any backup copies of these records must also adhere to encryption standards. Similarly, in the financial industry, encrypted backups are essential to secure financial records, customer information, and transactional data.

The process of encrypting backup data begins with choosing an encryption algorithm. There are several encryption algorithms available, each with varying levels of security and performance. One of the most widely used encryption standards is AES (Advanced Encryption Standard), specifically AES-256, which is known for its robust security and efficiency. AES-256 uses a 256-bit encryption key, making it highly resistant to brute-force attacks. It is often the preferred choice for encrypting sensitive data in backup systems due to its proven security and widespread support across various platforms and services. While AES-256 is considered highly secure, administrators should also consider using additional security measures, such as password protection and key management, to further strengthen the backup system.

Another important consideration in backup encryption is key management. The encryption key is the cornerstone of the encryption process, and the security of backup data relies on its protection. If the encryption key is lost or stolen, the encrypted data becomes inaccessible, rendering the backup useless. Proper key management ensures that encryption keys are securely stored, rotated, and accessed only by authorized individuals. Many encryption systems include features such as key escrow, where the key is stored in a secure location and can be retrieved only by trusted personnel. Additionally, it is essential to implement multi-factor authentication (MFA) when accessing the encryption key, ensuring that only authorized users can decrypt the backup data. Key management solutions can be centralized, allowing for more efficient management of encryption keys across multiple systems, or decentralized, where each system or backup device manages its own key.

For organizations using cloud-based backup solutions, encryption provides an additional layer of security for data in transit and at rest. Cloud storage providers typically offer server-side encryption, where data is encrypted before being stored in the cloud. However, to maximize security, it is advisable to encrypt the data on the client side before transmission, ensuring that the data is encrypted before it leaves the local environment. This approach, known as end-to-end encryption, prevents cloud providers or any unauthorized third parties from accessing the backup data. While this increases the security of cloud backups, it also places more responsibility on the organization to manage the encryption process and ensure that encryption keys are securely stored and protected.

In addition to encryption, backup systems should incorporate other security practices to protect against unauthorized access. Access control is a fundamental component of backup security, ensuring that only authorized users or administrators can initiate, modify, or restore backups. Role-based access control (RBAC) can be used to limit access to backup systems based on the user's role in the organization, ensuring that sensitive data is only accessible by those who need it to perform their job functions. Backup systems should also be configured to log access attempts and activities, allowing administrators to monitor and audit any suspicious activity. Regular audits of backup systems help to identify potential security gaps and ensure that the backup process is functioning as intended.

Network security is another critical factor when it comes to securing backup data, particularly when backups are transmitted over the internet or across untrusted networks. To protect backup data during transmission, it is essential to use secure communication protocols such as SSL/TLS (Secure Sockets Layer/Transport Layer Security) to encrypt the data while in transit. These protocols ensure that the data remains secure as it travels between the source and the backup destination, preventing eavesdropping or interception by malicious actors. In environments with high security requirements, it may be necessary to use a dedicated, private network for backup transfers, ensuring that the data is not exposed to external threats.

Another important security consideration is physical security. While backup encryption protects data in case of unauthorized digital access, physical security ensures that backup media—whether on external hard drives, tapes, or other physical storage devices—are not stolen, damaged, or lost. Storing backup media in a secure location, such as a locked cabinet or a climate-controlled facility, is essential to prevent physical theft or environmental damage. For off-site backups, such as those stored in a remote data center or cloud storage, ensuring that the data center itself is physically secure and protected from unauthorized access is equally important.

Despite these security measures, it is important to regularly test backup systems to ensure their reliability and effectiveness. Regular testing of backups, including verifying encryption, recovery processes, and data integrity, ensures that backup systems are functioning as intended and that data can be successfully restored when needed. This testing should be performed periodically, with different types of data and backup media, to ensure that the organization is prepared for any potential disaster recovery scenario.

As organizations rely more heavily on digital data, ensuring that backup systems are both secure and efficient has become a critical part of overall data protection strategies. Backup encryption plays an essential role in securing data and ensuring that it remains safe from unauthorized access. By using strong encryption methods, managing encryption keys properly, and combining these efforts with access controls, network security, and physical protection, organizations can ensure that their backup systems provide the necessary level of security. With the increasing sophistication of cyber threats, adopting a comprehensive security approach for backup solutions is not just a best practice, but a necessity for protecting critical data.

Disaster Recovery Planning and Backup Systems

Disaster recovery planning is a critical aspect of business continuity, aiming to ensure that an organization can recover and restore essential operations after an unforeseen event, such as a natural disaster, hardware failure, or cyberattack. At the core of disaster recovery planning is the ability to restore lost or damaged data quickly and efficiently. Backup systems play a pivotal role in this process, providing the means to safeguard data and ensure that it is available for recovery when needed. Without a reliable backup strategy, organizations risk losing valuable data, which could lead to operational disruption, financial losses, and a damaged reputation. Disaster recovery and backup systems must be integrated into a holistic approach that considers various factors, including risk assessment, recovery time objectives, and the type of backup solution used.

The first step in disaster recovery planning is conducting a comprehensive risk assessment. This involves identifying potential threats to the organization's data, systems, and infrastructure. These threats could range from natural disasters like floods, fires, or earthquakes, to cyber threats such as ransomware or data breaches. A thorough risk assessment helps organizations understand the likelihood and potential impact of each type of disaster, allowing them to prioritize their recovery efforts. Understanding these risks is crucial in determining how much data needs to be protected and the level of backup redundancy required. For example, organizations with critical data that must remain accessible at all times, such as healthcare or financial institutions, must plan for near-instant recovery, while other businesses may tolerate longer recovery times.

Once the risks are understood, organizations need to establish clear recovery objectives. Two key metrics in disaster recovery are the Recovery Time Objective (RTO) and the Recovery Point Objective (RPO). The RTO refers to the maximum acceptable downtime for a system or service before it affects the business, while the RPO defines the maximum acceptable amount of data loss, typically expressed in terms of time. For instance, a system with a short RTO might require a real-time or near-real-time backup system, ensuring that the data can be restored quickly, even in the event of a disaster. On the other hand, an organization with a longer RTO may be able to rely on less frequent backups. The RPO helps define how often backups should be taken and whether incremental or full backups are necessary to meet the organization's needs.

Backup systems form the backbone of a disaster recovery plan, as they are the primary mechanism for recovering data after a disaster. A well-designed backup system should incorporate redundancy, automation, security, and scalability. Redundancy ensures that there are multiple copies of critical data stored in different locations, such as on-premises, in remote data centers, or in the cloud. Redundant backups increase the chances of successfully recovering data, even if one backup copy is lost, corrupted, or inaccessible due to a disaster. Multiple backup locations, including off-site storage and cloud-based backups, further enhance the organization's ability to recover from a range of disasters, from hardware failures to large-scale regional outages.

Backup automation is another key component of disaster recovery planning. Manual backup processes are prone to errors and inconsistencies, potentially leaving critical data unprotected. Automating the backup process ensures that backups are taken regularly and without human intervention. Scheduled backups, for example, can be set to run daily, weekly, or even continuously, depending on the organization's needs. This automation also reduces the administrative burden, as system administrators do not need to manually initiate backups or verify their completion. With automated backups, organizations can be confident that their data is consistently being protected and that it is available for restoration in the event of a disaster.

Security is an essential consideration in both backup systems and disaster recovery planning. Backup data, especially when it is stored remotely or in the cloud, must be encrypted to prevent unauthorized access or tampering. Encryption protects backup data both during transmission and while at rest, ensuring that it remains secure even if it is intercepted or accessed by malicious actors. Along with encryption, access control mechanisms should be implemented to restrict who can access or modify backup data. Only authorized personnel should have the ability to initiate restores or manage backup configurations. Moreover, multi-factor authentication (MFA) should be used when accessing backup systems, adding an extra layer of protection to prevent unauthorized access.

In addition to security, backup systems should be designed for scalability. As organizations grow, so do their data storage needs. A backup solution that works well for a small business may not be suitable for a large enterprise with vast amounts of data. Scalable backup systems, such as cloud-based solutions, can expand as needed, allowing organizations to add storage capacity without significant upfront investment in physical infrastructure. Cloud backups, in particular, offer flexibility by enabling businesses to pay only for the storage they use, while also providing the ability to scale quickly as data volumes increase.

Once the backup system is in place, it is essential to regularly test the disaster recovery plan to ensure its effectiveness. Backup testing involves verifying that backups are complete, intact, and recoverable. Regularly testing restores, whether it is restoring a small file or a complete system, ensures that the backup data is valid and can be successfully used to recover from a disaster. Testing also helps identify any weaknesses in the backup process, such as missing files, failed backups, or slow recovery times. Testing should be done on a regular basis, ideally as part of the organization's routine disaster recovery drills. By conducting these tests, organizations can ensure that their backup systems will function as expected during an actual disaster.

Additionally, disaster recovery planning should involve clear communication protocols. In the event of a disaster, all relevant personnel should know their roles and responsibilities in executing the recovery plan. Having predefined communication channels and detailed procedures ensures that the recovery process can be initiated quickly, minimizing downtime and the impact on operations. Documentation is also a critical part of disaster recovery planning. Backup schedules, recovery procedures, and contact information for key personnel should be clearly documented and easily accessible. This documentation can be invaluable in a high-stress situation, ensuring that everyone involved in the recovery process understands their responsibilities and how to proceed.

As businesses rely more heavily on digital infrastructure, the importance of disaster recovery planning and backup systems cannot be overstated. A well-constructed backup system is not just about protecting data—it is about ensuring that an organization can quickly resume its operations after a disaster, reducing the financial, operational, and reputational damage caused by data loss or extended downtime. A comprehensive disaster recovery plan, supported by a robust and secure backup system, is an essential investment for businesses of all sizes, helping them prepare for the unexpected and maintain business continuity in the face of challenges.

Restoring Filesystems from Backup

Restoring filesystems from backup is an essential part of any data protection strategy. Whether due to hardware failure, accidental deletion, corruption, or a disaster recovery scenario, having the ability to restore filesystems efficiently and accurately ensures business continuity and reduces downtime. A robust backup strategy is only as good as the restore process it supports, as it is during restoration that an organization's true resilience is tested. Effective restoration involves understanding the backup architecture, the tools used for the process, and the potential risks and challenges associated with data recovery. It requires careful planning, testing, and sometimes troubleshooting to ensure that the restoration process meets the organization's recovery objectives and restores data accurately.

The first step in restoring a filesystem is to assess the backup data to determine what type of backup was performed, when it was performed, and whether the data is intact and available for recovery. Filesystem backups can be full, incremental, or differential, and each type affects the restoration process in different ways. A full backup contains a complete copy of the filesystem at a specific point in time, so it can be restored without needing any additional backup data. However, restoring from full backups can be more time-consuming and storage-intensive compared to incremental or differential backups. Incremental backups, on the other hand, only store the changes made since the last backup, meaning that a full restore will require applying the last full backup along with each incremental backup made since then. Differential backups store changes made since the last full backup, which simplifies the restore process compared to incremental backups but may require more storage and bandwidth as they accumulate over time.

Once the backup type is identified, administrators must ensure that the correct backup data is selected for restoration. This often requires knowing the exact point in time to which the filesystem needs to be restored. In some cases, organizations might need to restore the system to a specific date and time to avoid issues caused by recent changes, such as the introduction of malware or corruption. In other cases, it might be necessary to restore to the most recent backup to minimize data loss. Having a well-documented backup and restore procedure, including timestamps and versioning, ensures that administrators can quickly identify the correct backup set to use.

When initiating the restore process, it is important to consider the tools and utilities available to handle the restoration. Different operating systems and backup solutions offer different methods for restoring filesystems. On Linux systems, tools such as rsync, tar, or specialized backup software like Bacula or Amanda may be used for filesystem restoration. These tools typically provide flexibility in restoring entire filesystems or individual files and directories. For example, rsync allows for efficient restoration of data by only copying files that have changed, ensuring a faster and more efficient recovery process. Similarly, tar is often used for restoring compressed archives created during backup. On Windows systems, utilities like Windows Server Backup or third-party solutions like Veeam and Acronis offer graphical interfaces for restoring filesystems, simplifying the process for administrators who may not be familiar with command-line tools.

One of the most critical aspects of restoring filesystems is ensuring that the restoration is complete and accurate. Incomplete or corrupted restores can lead to system instability, data corruption, or loss of vital files. To avoid this, administrators should verify the integrity of the backup data before beginning the restoration process. This can be done by performing checksum comparisons between the backup and the source filesystem or using built-in verification tools that many backup systems provide. Once the restoration process begins, monitoring tools should be used to track the progress of the restore and ensure that no errors occur during the process. If errors are detected, they should be addressed immediately to prevent incomplete restores.

Another important factor to consider during the restoration process is the hardware environment. When restoring filesystems, it is critical that the hardware being used matches the configuration of the original system, or that the restoration process is tailored to accommodate differences in the hardware. For instance, if the filesystem is being restored to a new server with different disk configurations or hardware components, compatibility issues may arise. This could include differences in partition tables, disk layouts, or even file system types. Administrators may need to perform additional configuration steps to align the filesystem restoration with the new hardware, such as resizing partitions, modifying configuration files, or adjusting disk alignment.

In virtualized environments, restoring filesystems can be more complex due to the abstracted nature of the underlying infrastructure. Virtual machines (VMs) often require specific restoration tools and processes to restore both the virtual disk and the VM configuration to their previous state. Backup solutions designed for virtualized environments, such as Veeam or VMware's vSphere Data Protection, typically offer integrated restore options that account for the entire VM, ensuring that the restored virtual machine operates as expected. It is crucial to ensure that the VM's disk layout, network configurations, and other system settings are correctly restored to avoid issues with system functionality.

Network bandwidth is also an important consideration when restoring filesystems from remote backups, especially in large-scale environments with significant amounts of data. Restoring large datasets over the network can lead to extended downtime, particularly if the available bandwidth is limited. To mitigate this, administrators may need to optimize network performance during the restore process. Techniques such as bandwidth throttling or scheduling restores during off-peak hours can help reduce the impact on network performance. Additionally, some backup solutions support incremental restoration, which allows for partial restoration of data, reducing the time required to restore the system and enabling a quicker return to operational status.

For businesses relying on cloud backups, the restoration process may introduce additional challenges. Cloud restores can be slower than on-site restores due to the dependence on internet bandwidth and cloud storage performance. Cloud storage providers often offer options for expedited recovery, such as using high-performance storage tiers or providing physical devices for initial data transfer. These options can help mitigate the challenges of long recovery times but may incur additional costs. Additionally, organizations should ensure that they understand the recovery process provided by their cloud storage provider, as cloud-based restoration workflows can differ from traditional on-premises restoration.

Data consistency is another concern when restoring filesystems. In environments where the filesystem is part of a larger application or database infrastructure, administrators must ensure that the data being restored is consistent with the state of other systems. For example, restoring a database without restoring its associated transaction logs can result in data inconsistency and errors. Many modern backup solutions offer application-aware backups, which ensure that backups are taken in a way that preserves the consistency of application data, including databases and virtual machines. These solutions can also automate the process of restoring databases or applications to a consistent state, simplifying the recovery process.

After the restoration is complete, it is essential to perform thorough testing to ensure that the system is fully operational. This includes checking the integrity of the restored files, ensuring that system configurations are correct, and verifying that applications and services are running as expected. The testing phase is vital to identify any issues that may have arisen during the restore process, such as missing files, configuration errors, or network connectivity problems.

Restoring filesystems from backup is a critical skill for system administrators, requiring both technical expertise and careful planning. A successful restoration ensures that organizations can recover from data loss or system failures without major disruptions. By understanding the tools, processes, and potential challenges involved in filesystem restoration, administrators can develop effective recovery strategies that minimize downtime and ensure that systems are quickly returned to a fully functional state. Through thorough preparation, regular testing, and continuous monitoring, organizations can ensure that their restore processes are reliable and effective, even in the face of unexpected disasters.

Snapshot-Based Backup Techniques

Snapshot-based backup techniques have become increasingly popular in modern data protection strategies due to their ability to provide fast, efficient, and consistent backups of entire filesystems or individual volumes. A snapshot is a point-in-time copy of a filesystem or data volume that captures the state of the system at that exact moment. Unlike traditional backup methods that copy all data, snapshots create a record of changes, which allows for rapid backup processes with minimal impact on system performance. This technique is particularly useful in environments where data is constantly changing or in high-availability systems that require minimal downtime during backups.

The fundamental advantage of snapshot-based backups is speed. Traditional backups often involve copying large amounts of data from one location to another, which can be time-consuming and resource-intensive. In contrast, a snapshot is a much quicker operation, typically requiring only a small amount of time to create. This is because a snapshot does not immediately copy the data but instead records the state of the system and tracks any changes that occur after the snapshot is taken. Snapshots work by utilizing a copy-on-write or redirect-on-write method. In copy-on-write, the system creates a snapshot and marks the current state of the data, but only stores the modified data as changes occur. In redirect-on-write, the system writes changes to a different location, leaving the original data untouched. Both methods allow the snapshot to be created almost instantly, which significantly reduces backup times compared to traditional methods.

Snapshots are typically implemented in storage systems that support advanced features such as logical volume managers (LVM), file system snapshots, or hardware-based storage solutions. Many modern file systems, such as ZFS, Btrfs, and NTFS, offer built-in snapshot capabilities. These file systems can quickly create snapshots of volumes or file systems without interrupting normal system operations. For instance, ZFS provides snapshot functionality that allows administrators to create and restore snapshots of entire datasets or specific filesystems. This built-in support makes it easy to integrate snapshot-based backup techniques into existing storage environments, without needing additional backup software or hardware.

One of the key features of snapshot-based backups is their ability to provide consistency. When creating a snapshot, the data is captured in a stable state, even if the data is actively being written to at the time the snapshot is taken. In contrast, traditional backups may capture files in a partially written state, which can lead to inconsistencies or corruption when the data is restored. This is particularly important in environments where applications and databases are constantly changing, such as in online transaction processing (OLTP) systems or web applications. A snapshot ensures that the data captured is consistent and can be restored to its exact state at the time of the snapshot, without the need to perform complex recovery procedures to handle partial writes.

For databases, snapshot-based backups are especially beneficial. Many modern databases, including Oracle, MySQL, and Microsoft SQL Server, can use snapshots to create consistent backup copies of active database systems without interrupting database operations. When a snapshot is taken, the database continues to run normally, processing transactions and updates. Once the snapshot is created, administrators can proceed with backing up the snapshot without affecting database performance or availability. This method ensures that the backup copy is consistent with the actual data in the database, including all the changes made during the snapshot process. As a result, snapshot-based backups are a preferred solution in environments where downtime is not acceptable, and data consistency is critical.

Another advantage of snapshot-based backups is the ability to perform quick restores. Since a snapshot represents a point-in-time copy of the data, restoring from a snapshot can be done quickly, often in a matter of seconds or minutes. This is in stark contrast to traditional backup methods, where the restoration process can be slow and cumbersome, especially for large datasets. With snapshots, administrators can easily revert a filesystem or database to its previous state by simply restoring the snapshot. This process is particularly useful in disaster recovery scenarios, where minimizing downtime is essential for maintaining business operations. Restoring from a snapshot is also less resource-intensive than restoring from a traditional backup, which requires copying large amounts of data back onto the system.

Snapshot-based backups also offer flexibility in terms of backup frequency and retention. Since snapshots are created quickly and do not involve copying large amounts of data, administrators can take snapshots frequently, ensuring that data is protected with minimal impact on system performance. For example, it is not uncommon for businesses to take multiple snapshots throughout the day, ensuring that the data is up-to-date without overloading the system or requiring long backup windows. Snapshots can also be retained for varying periods, depending on the organization's needs. Older snapshots can be deleted or archived to secondary storage, ensuring that storage resources are managed efficiently. Furthermore, since snapshots capture the state of the data at a specific point in time, they allow for easy versioning and recovery of previous states of the data, which can be useful for identifying and correcting errors or recovering from data corruption.

Despite their many advantages, snapshot-based backups do come with some considerations. One of the main concerns is the use of storage space. While snapshots are efficient in terms of speed and performance, they still consume storage resources, especially when multiple snapshots are taken or when snapshots are kept for long periods. Over time, as more snapshots accumulate, the storage requirements can increase significantly. This is particularly true in environments with large datasets or high-frequency snapshot schedules. To manage this, administrators must monitor storage usage and implement retention policies that balance the need for frequent backups with available storage resources. Some storage systems provide automated tools for managing snapshot lifecycles, including deleting older snapshots or moving them to lower-cost storage tiers.

Another consideration is the potential for performance degradation when using snapshots, particularly in systems with limited resources. While snapshots are designed to be lightweight and efficient, the process of writing changes to the underlying storage can introduce some overhead. For example, if a system is heavily utilized and many snapshots are created, the storage system may experience performance issues due to the increased I/O operations associated with tracking changes. This can impact the overall performance of the system, particularly for applications or services that rely on high-speed disk access. To mitigate these issues, administrators should carefully manage the frequency of snapshots, optimize storage configurations, and monitor system performance regularly.

Snapshot-based backups also require a robust recovery strategy. Although snapshots provide fast restores, administrators must ensure that the snapshots are being properly backed up and that they can be restored in case of a disaster. Many organizations implement a hybrid backup approach, where snapshots are used for frequent, short-term backups, and traditional backups are used for long-term data protection. By combining these methods, businesses can achieve both the speed and efficiency of snapshot-based backups with the reliability and completeness of traditional backups.

Snapshot-based backup techniques have become an integral part of modern data protection strategies. Their speed, efficiency, and ability to maintain data consistency make them an ideal solution for environments that require minimal downtime and reliable data recovery. As businesses continue to face increasing amounts of data and more complex IT infrastructures, snapshot-based backups will remain a crucial tool for ensuring data availability and minimizing the risk of data loss. With proper management, snapshot-based backups can provide a fast, flexible, and secure means of protecting valuable data.

Backup Testing: Ensuring Integrity and Reliability

Backup testing is an often-overlooked yet crucial aspect of data protection. While many organizations focus on creating backup systems and schedules, ensuring that those backups are reliable and can be restored when necessary is just as important. The integrity and reliability of backup data can only be confirmed through systematic testing. Without adequate testing, organizations are exposed to significant risks, as they might be unaware of corrupted, incomplete, or inaccessible backups until they attempt a recovery in a critical situation. Backup testing helps verify that the data stored in backup systems is intact, usable, and accessible in the event of data loss, system failure, or disaster recovery. Regular testing ensures that backup processes are functioning as expected and guarantees that data can be reliably restored when needed.

The first step in backup testing is verifying that backups are being performed correctly. A backup process might be scheduled and automated, but testing ensures that these processes are indeed capturing the correct data at the right intervals. For instance, it is essential to confirm that the intended directories, databases, or virtual machines are included in the backup set. If a backup system is not set up correctly, it may fail to capture important files or data, leaving gaps that could become critical in a disaster scenario. Testing helps identify and correct configuration errors, ensuring that backup schedules are aligned with the organization's needs and that no important data is missed.

Once the backup process has been verified, the next critical step is testing the integrity of the backup data. Integrity testing involves checking that the data in the backup is not corrupted or damaged. Over time, backup media can deteriorate, or storage systems may develop faults that lead to data corruption. A corrupted backup is as useless as no backup at all, as it cannot be relied upon for recovery. By performing integrity checks, organizations can ensure that the backup files are intact and have not been compromised by issues such as disk failures, network errors during backup transfers, or software bugs in the backup tool. Many backup software solutions provide built-in integrity checking mechanisms that calculate checksums or hash values for backup files, which can be used to verify data integrity during the testing process.

Another important aspect of backup testing is verifying the restoration process itself. A backup is only useful if it can be restored successfully when required, so organizations must regularly test the ability to restore data from backups. This involves not only ensuring that the data can be recovered but also testing the actual process of restoring files or entire systems. Testing the restoration process ensures that the recovery procedure is efficient and straightforward. During the testing, administrators should simulate real-world scenarios by restoring files to their original location or to a different machine to verify that the data is correctly restored. By conducting periodic restoration tests, organizations can ensure that the recovery process will run smoothly when it's needed most, minimizing downtime during an actual disaster recovery situation.

Restoration testing should be done on various types of data to ensure that all files, applications, and systems can be recovered properly. This includes verifying the restoration of both individual files and entire systems, ensuring that no data is lost in the process. For example, it's crucial to test the restoration of database systems, virtual machines, and application data, as these types of data can be more complex to restore than simple file systems. Testing should also involve restoring to different environments, such as new hardware or virtualized platforms, to ensure that data can be successfully recovered in various scenarios.

Backup testing also extends to the timing and efficiency of the recovery process. In many businesses, rapid recovery is a key requirement to ensure minimal disruption to operations. Backup testing can be used to measure how long it takes to restore data, as well as how long it takes to bring the system back to a fully operational state. For example, if a company needs to restore a large database, it's essential to know how long that recovery will take and whether it fits within the acceptable recovery time objective (RTO). If recovery times are too long, the organization may need to optimize its backup and recovery strategy, perhaps by switching to faster storage systems or by employing more efficient backup methods, such as incremental backups or snapshot-based backups.

Along with testing the recovery speed, it's important to evaluate the backup's effectiveness across different types of failures. Testing should encompass a variety of failure scenarios to ensure that the backup system is robust enough to handle them. For instance, an organization might test recovery after a hardware failure, such as a hard disk crash, or a system crash, where an entire operating system must be restored. In a disaster recovery scenario, backups might need to be restored from a remote location, so testing should also involve testing the retrieval process from off-site backups, including cloud-based or remote storage backups. These tests ensure that all components of the backup and recovery system are functioning correctly, regardless of the failure scenario.

It's also vital that backup testing includes an evaluation of the backup storage media itself. Over time, storage devices like tapes, disks, or cloud-based storage can become corrupted, worn out, or unreliable. Performing periodic testing of storage devices ensures that the backup media remains viable and that data can be retrieved as expected. Regular testing of storage media, especially for systems using physical storage such as tape backups or external hard drives, helps identify when media degradation occurs. For cloud storage, organizations should test both the retrieval speed and data integrity to ensure that data can be restored quickly and accurately when needed.

Backup testing should not be a one-time or sporadic activity but an ongoing process that is incorporated into regular IT maintenance practices. In fact, backup testing should be done as part of a broader disaster recovery or business continuity testing program. As organizations scale and evolve, their data protection needs will change, so backup systems and recovery processes should be periodically reviewed and tested to ensure they align with current requirements. The frequency of backup tests depends on the size and complexity of the organization, but it is typically recommended to test backups at least quarterly, with more frequent tests for critical systems.

Furthermore, backup testing should be documented thoroughly, with records of the results, including any issues encountered and how they were resolved. Detailed records allow organizations to track the effectiveness of their backup strategy over time and ensure that lessons learned from previous tests are applied to improve future backup and recovery processes. This documentation can also serve as an audit trail for compliance purposes, particularly in industries with strict regulatory requirements, such as finance and healthcare.

Regular backup testing is essential to ensure that backup systems are functioning as intended, and that the organization can recover its critical data quickly and efficiently in the event of a disaster. While performing backups regularly is vital, ensuring that those backups are valid, intact, and recoverable is just as important. Through comprehensive and ongoing testing, businesses can reduce the risk of data loss, minimize downtime, and maintain operational continuity in the face of unforeseen events. As organizations grow and become more reliant on data, backup testing is an integral part of maintaining the integrity and reliability of their backup systems.

Managing Backup Storage Devices and Media

Managing backup storage devices and media is a critical aspect of any organization's data protection strategy. The reliability, security, and performance of backup systems depend heavily on the type of storage devices used and how well they are maintained. Whether an organization relies on traditional magnetic tape, hard drives, or modern cloud-based storage, the way backup media is managed can significantly impact the overall effectiveness of the backup and recovery process. Proper management involves not only selecting the right storage devices but also ensuring that the backup media is configured, stored, and monitored in a way that ensures data integrity and availability in case of a disaster.

The first consideration when managing backup storage devices is choosing the appropriate media for the organization's specific needs. Different types of storage media offer various benefits in terms of cost, capacity, speed, and longevity. For instance, tape drives have traditionally been used for long-term storage due to their high capacity and relatively low cost per gigabyte. While tape storage remains a reliable option for archival backups, it can be slower and more cumbersome compared to modern alternatives. In contrast, hard disk drives (HDDs) and solid-state drives (SSDs) offer faster data transfer rates and are more suitable for frequent backups and quicker restores, making them ideal for environments with high data change rates or where minimal downtime is required during restoration. Each type of media must be evaluated for its performance characteristics and how they align with the organization's recovery objectives and available budget.

Cloud storage is increasingly becoming a popular choice for backup media, particularly in businesses that require scalable storage solutions with off-site redundancy. Cloud backup services allow organizations to store backup data off-site, ensuring protection from local disasters like fires or floods. Cloud solutions can also be highly flexible, offering pay-as-you-go pricing models and the ability to scale storage resources as needed. However, cloud storage introduces new considerations such as data retrieval times, bandwidth requirements, and security concerns, which must be addressed during the management process. For example, while cloud storage offers excellent scalability and redundancy, the cost of large-scale cloud storage can increase rapidly over time, especially if the data is not efficiently managed or if retention policies are not optimized.

Once the appropriate backup media has been chosen, the next step is to establish an effective storage management policy. One of the most important aspects of managing backup media is ensuring that the storage devices are properly configured and organized. This includes setting up logical volumes, partitioning disks effectively, and ensuring that data is stored in an organized manner that facilitates quick retrieval during restoration. Disk-based backup systems, whether using local storage or network-attached storage (NAS), should be configured to use RAID (Redundant Array of Independent Disks) for redundancy and fault tolerance. RAID allows data to be striped across multiple disks or mirrored for greater reliability, reducing the risk of data loss due to a single disk failure. Storage systems should also be organized with clear labeling and folder structures to ensure that backup data is easy to locate and retrieve in case of a disaster.

In addition to physical organization, it is important to manage the lifecycle of backup media effectively. Backup retention policies are crucial to maintaining an efficient and cost-effective backup environment. Over time, backup media can accumulate, leading to excessive storage costs and inefficient management practices. Retention policies should define how long backups are retained before they are deleted, archived, or overwritten. Organizations must consider factors such as regulatory compliance, business requirements, and the frequency of data changes when designing retention policies. For example, some industries may require that backups be kept for several years for compliance purposes, while others may have less stringent requirements. By setting clear retention policies and automating the backup process, organizations can ensure that they are retaining only the data that is needed while minimizing the amount of unused or obsolete backup media.

Physical storage management is also critical for ensuring the long-term integrity of backup media. Backup devices, particularly physical storage media like tapes, disks, and hard drives, are susceptible to wear and environmental damage. Proper storage conditions are essential for preserving the longevity and reliability of backup media. Tapes, for example, should be stored in climate-controlled environments to prevent deterioration due to humidity and temperature fluctuations. Hard drives should be stored in protective enclosures to prevent physical damage from impacts, dust, or static electricity. Furthermore, regular checks of backup media should be performed to detect any signs of failure, such as disk errors, read/write failures, or the degradation of tape quality over time.

Off-site backup storage is another crucial consideration, especially in scenarios where on-site data is vulnerable to local disasters. Off-site storage solutions, such as remote data centers or cloud storage, provide additional redundancy and protection for backup data. When using off-site storage, it is important to ensure that backup data is securely transmitted and stored. This involves encrypting the backup data during transit to protect it from unauthorized access and ensuring that the storage provider follows best practices for data security and redundancy. Additionally, access controls should be implemented to limit who can access or modify backup data, both on-site and off-site.

Backup testing is an often-neglected but vital part of managing backup media. Regularly testing backup media ensures that the backup process is working as expected and that the data can be reliably restored in the event of a failure. Without testing, an organization might not discover that its backup media is faulty or that its restoration process is flawed until it's too late. Backup testing involves both verifying the integrity of the stored data and performing actual restoration exercises to ensure that the data can be successfully retrieved and used. These tests should be done periodically and include tests of both full and incremental backups to ensure that both types of backups function as expected.

Security is an integral part of managing backup storage devices and media. Backups contain critical data, and their protection is just as important as the security of primary data. Backup media should be encrypted to prevent unauthorized access, especially when backups are stored off-site or in the cloud. Encryption ensures that even if backup media is lost or stolen, the data remains inaccessible to malicious actors. Access control mechanisms should also be in place to restrict who can access backup devices, particularly physical devices like tapes or external hard drives. Strong authentication methods, such as multi-factor authentication, should be used when accessing cloud or network-based backup systems to ensure that only authorized users can initiate restores or modify backup settings.

Ultimately, managing backup storage devices and media involves a combination of selecting the right storage solutions, organizing and configuring them effectively, and maintaining their integrity and security over time. By adopting a proactive approach to backup media management, organizations can ensure that their backup systems are reliable, cost-effective, and secure. Regular monitoring, testing, and adherence to best practices will ensure that backup media remains functional and that data can be restored quickly and accurately in the event of a failure. Proper backup storage management not only helps protect valuable data but also enhances the organization's overall disaster recovery capabilities, ensuring business continuity even in the face of unexpected events.

Automation Tools for Backup Management

Automation tools have revolutionized the way backup management is performed, making it easier for organizations to ensure data protection, reduce manual effort, and eliminate human error. Backup management is a critical function within any IT infrastructure, as data loss can result in significant downtime, financial losses, and reputational damage. However, managing backup systems manually can be time-consuming, prone to mistakes, and inefficient. As data volumes grow and the complexity of IT environments increases, automation tools have become indispensable in streamlining backup processes and ensuring that backup operations are carried out efficiently, reliably, and consistently. These tools can handle everything from scheduling and executing backups to monitoring and verifying the integrity of backup data, significantly improving the overall backup strategy.

The core function of backup automation tools is to schedule and execute backup tasks automatically without requiring constant manual intervention. Scheduling backups ensures that data is consistently protected and that the backups occur at predetermined times, such as during off-peak hours when system usage is minimal. This minimizes disruption to normal operations and helps avoid performance slowdowns that may occur when backups are manually initiated during busy hours. Automation tools enable IT administrators to define the frequency of backups, whether they are daily, weekly, or monthly, as well as determine the type of backup (full, incremental, or differential) based on the organization's needs. This ability to automate backups eliminates the risk of forgetting to initiate a backup, ensuring that data protection is always up-to-date.

In addition to scheduling, backup automation tools can streamline the process of backing up various types of data across multiple systems, locations, and platforms. Modern IT environments often involve complex setups, such as virtual machines, cloud services, databases, and on-premises file systems, which require backup solutions that can handle diverse workloads. Automation tools can be configured to back up data from different sources, ensuring that all systems, including critical applications and data, are included in the backup process. Furthermore, automation tools can support centralized management, where administrators can monitor and configure backup jobs across multiple servers or locations from a single interface. This is especially useful in large organizations with distributed infrastructures, as it simplifies the backup management process and ensures consistent protection across the entire environment.

Another key advantage of backup automation tools is the ability to monitor backup jobs in real-time and provide alerts in case of failures or issues. Automation tools track the progress of backup tasks and can immediately notify administrators if a backup job fails or encounters errors. This proactive monitoring allows administrators to address potential issues before they escalate into larger problems. For example, if a backup job fails due to insufficient storage space or network connectivity issues, an automated tool can alert the IT team to take corrective action. In addition to error notifications, automation tools can generate detailed logs and reports that provide insight into the status of backup tasks, helping administrators identify trends, troubleshoot issues, and improve the overall reliability of the backup system.

Backup automation tools also play a critical role in verifying the integrity of backups. Simply running a backup job does not guarantee that the backup data is complete, accurate, or recoverable. Integrity verification ensures that the backup data is intact and can be restored without issues. Many automation tools include built-in functionality to verify the integrity of backups during or after the backup process. This verification process typically involves comparing checksums or hashes of the original data and the backup data, ensuring that the backup is a true copy of the source data. If discrepancies are detected, the system can alert the administrator and, in some cases, automatically retry the backup or attempt to fix the issue. This capability is essential in preventing data corruption or incomplete backups, which could undermine the recovery process in a disaster.

Automation tools can also simplify the process of backup retention and management, which is essential for reducing storage costs and ensuring compliance with data retention policies. Retention management involves determining how long backup data should be stored before being deleted, archived, or overwritten. Automated tools can be configured to implement retention policies that automatically delete old backups, archive them to secondary storage, or move them to a more cost-effective storage tier, such as cold storage or tape. By automating retention management, organizations can ensure that they do not exceed their storage limits, while still retaining the necessary backups for compliance or business continuity purposes. This also reduces the administrative burden of manually managing backup data and allows IT teams to focus on other tasks.

Cloud backup solutions, in particular, benefit greatly from automation tools. With cloud backups, organizations can leverage off-site storage for data protection, which helps mitigate the risk of local disasters. However, managing cloud backups manually can be cumbersome, especially when dealing with large amounts of data or a large number of cloud storage accounts. Automation tools can handle cloud backup scheduling, monitoring, and reporting across multiple cloud platforms, allowing organizations to manage their cloud-based backups from a single interface. These tools can also integrate with various cloud providers, enabling administrators to manage data storage across different regions or environments. Additionally, automation tools can optimize bandwidth usage during cloud backups by compressing and deduplicating data before it is transferred, making the backup process more efficient and cost-effective.

For organizations using virtualized environments, backup automation tools offer specialized features to back up virtual machines (VMs) and their associated data. Virtualized environments require consistent and reliable backups to ensure that entire VMs, along with their configurations and data, can be restored quickly. Automation tools can integrate with virtualization platforms such as VMware or Microsoft Hyper-V to automate the backup of VMs. These tools can be configured to back up individual VMs, specific VM snapshots, or entire virtualized environments. They can also perform application-aware backups to ensure that database files and other active data are captured in a consistent state, preventing potential data corruption or downtime during restores.

Backup automation tools also help streamline the disaster recovery process by enabling rapid and reliable data restoration. In the event of a disaster, the ability to restore data quickly and accurately is crucial for minimizing downtime and ensuring business continuity. Automation tools can be used to create recovery workflows that define the steps required to restore data to a specific point in time. These workflows can be automated to ensure that the correct backup data is restored to the right systems, reducing the time and effort needed to recover from a failure. Additionally, some tools offer features like bare-metal restores, which enable organizations to recover entire systems, including the operating system, applications, and data, to new hardware without the need for manual configuration.

One of the significant challenges in managing backups is ensuring that backup processes are secure. Automation tools can enhance backup security by integrating encryption features that protect backup data during storage and transit. Data encryption ensures that even if backup data is stolen or accessed by unauthorized parties, it remains unreadable. Automation tools can manage encryption keys, implement access controls, and enforce policies that ensure only authorized users can access or modify backup data. Furthermore, automation tools can integrate with identity management systems to enable multi-factor authentication, adding an additional layer of protection to backup operations.

Backup automation tools are indispensable in modern data protection strategies, offering benefits such as efficient scheduling, monitoring, verification, retention management, and security. By automating routine backup tasks, organizations can reduce the risk of human error, ensure that backup processes are performed consistently, and focus more on strategic tasks. These tools not only make backup management more efficient but also help ensure that data can be restored quickly and reliably in the event of a failure, minimizing downtime and supporting business continuity. With the increasing complexity of IT environments and growing data volumes, backup automation tools are essential for organizations to maintain effective and reliable data protection systems.

Backup Monitoring and Alerting Systems

Backup monitoring and alerting systems play a crucial role in ensuring that backup processes are running smoothly and that potential issues are detected and addressed promptly. The integrity and availability of backup data are essential for disaster recovery and business continuity, and without proper monitoring, backup systems can fail silently, leaving organizations vulnerable to data loss. Effective backup monitoring provides visibility into the health of backup operations, while alerting systems ensure that administrators are informed of any issues in real time, enabling them to take corrective actions before small problems escalate into significant failures. These systems are essential for maintaining the reliability of backup infrastructures and ensuring that data is recoverable when needed.

One of the core functions of backup monitoring systems is tracking the status of backup jobs. Regular backups are critical to maintaining up-to-date copies of data, and monitoring these jobs ensures that they are completed successfully. Monitoring tools track the progress of each backup, checking whether the backup process was initiated, whether data was transferred successfully, and whether the backup finished without errors. This continuous tracking allows administrators to see at a glance whether backups are occurring as scheduled and whether there are any failures or delays. A failure in one backup job might go unnoticed without proper monitoring, but an effective backup monitoring system immediately flags such issues, helping administrators stay on top of the backup process.

Beyond tracking the status of backup jobs, backup monitoring systems also provide valuable insights into the overall performance of the backup infrastructure. They can monitor various performance metrics, such as backup speed, storage utilization, and network bandwidth usage. These metrics are crucial for identifying potential bottlenecks or inefficiencies in the backup process. For example, if backups are taking longer than expected, it could indicate a problem with storage performance, network congestion, or an inefficient backup configuration. Monitoring tools can help pinpoint the cause of delays, enabling administrators to optimize the backup system for better performance. Additionally, monitoring tools can track trends in storage usage, alerting administrators when storage space is running low, allowing them to take proactive measures such as expanding storage or implementing data deduplication techniques to reduce storage consumption.

Alerting systems are an essential component of backup monitoring, as they notify administrators of any issues or failures in real time. Without alerts, administrators might only discover a problem after a significant amount of time has passed, making it more difficult to address the issue and recover the data. Alerting systems are designed to send notifications when certain conditions are met, such as when a backup job fails, when there are insufficient resources (such as disk space or network bandwidth), or when backup data is corrupted. Alerts can be customized to fit the needs of the organization, allowing administrators to define the thresholds at which alerts are triggered. For example, an administrator might set an alert for when a backup job exceeds a certain time limit, or when the backup of critical files fails to complete successfully.

Alerts can be delivered through various communication channels, such as email, SMS, or integration with other monitoring platforms, such as Slack or PagerDuty. By having real-time notifications sent directly to the relevant personnel, organizations can ensure that backup issues are addressed promptly, minimizing downtime and the risk of data loss. The effectiveness of alerting systems depends on the accuracy and specificity of the notifications. Generic alerts that simply report "backup failed" might not provide enough information for administrators to quickly diagnose the problem. Advanced backup monitoring and alerting systems often provide detailed error messages, logs, and diagnostic information that help administrators understand the root cause of the issue, enabling them to take appropriate corrective actions. Additionally, alerts can be prioritized based on severity, ensuring that critical issues are addressed before less urgent ones.

Backup monitoring and alerting systems also play a key role in ensuring compliance with data protection regulations and organizational policies. Many industries are subject to strict data retention and backup requirements, such as healthcare (HIPAA), finance (PCI-DSS), or government sectors (GDPR). Backup systems must not only perform reliably but also maintain compliance with these regulations. Monitoring tools can provide reports that track backup activities, including the completion of backups, retention policies, and data access. These reports can be used to demonstrate compliance during audits or to ensure that backup policies are being followed correctly. For instance, if an organization is required to retain backups for a specific period, monitoring tools can track the age of backup data and send alerts when data is approaching the end of its retention period. This ensures that backups are properly archived or deleted in accordance with legal requirements, preventing data from being prematurely discarded or retained beyond its useful life.

As backup environments become more complex, with the increasing use of cloud storage, hybrid environments, and virtualized infrastructures, backup monitoring and alerting systems must be capable of handling diverse configurations. Cloud-based backup systems, for instance, may require different monitoring techniques than on-premises backup systems. Monitoring tools must be able to track the health of both local and remote backups, ensuring that data stored in the cloud is also backed up correctly and that cloud-based backup jobs are running efficiently. Hybrid environments that combine both on-premises and cloud storage require backup monitoring solutions that can seamlessly integrate and provide a unified view of the backup status across the entire infrastructure. Additionally, as more organizations rely on virtualization technologies such as VMware or Hyper-V, backup monitoring tools must support the monitoring of virtualized environments, including virtual machine (VM) backups and snapshots. Ensuring the integrity of virtualized backups requires specialized monitoring capabilities to track the status of virtual disks and VMs, as well as to ensure that backup processes do not interfere with ongoing virtual machine operations.

A key benefit of advanced backup monitoring systems is their ability to integrate with broader IT management tools. Many organizations use comprehensive monitoring platforms that track all aspects of the IT environment, from network performance to server health. By integrating backup monitoring into these platforms, administrators can gain a holistic view of their infrastructure's health and quickly identify any areas that require attention. Integration with broader monitoring tools allows backup issues to be correlated with other system events, such as network congestion or storage device failures, helping administrators to troubleshoot problems more effectively. This integration also streamlines the management of backup systems, as administrators can access backup data alongside other critical systems and services.

Regularly reviewing and fine-tuning backup monitoring and alerting systems is essential for maintaining an effective backup strategy. As organizations grow and their IT environments become more complex, backup requirements change, and new issues may arise. For example, an increase in data volume or the introduction of new applications may require adjustments to backup schedules, storage resources, or monitoring thresholds. Backup monitoring systems must evolve to reflect these changes, ensuring that the organization continues to meet its backup objectives and minimize risk. Regular testing of the monitoring and alerting system also helps to verify that alerts are being triggered correctly, and that the necessary personnel are receiving the notifications in a timely manner.

Backup monitoring and alerting systems are indispensable tools in modern data protection strategies. They provide the oversight necessary to ensure that backup operations run smoothly, that potential issues are identified early, and that data can be restored reliably when needed. By integrating robust monitoring and alerting systems into their backup infrastructure, organizations can ensure that their data protection strategies remain reliable, efficient, and compliant with regulatory requirements. These systems reduce the risk of data loss, improve recovery times, and contribute to the overall resilience of the organization's IT environment.

Using Versioning and Backup Catalogs

Versioning and backup catalogs are crucial tools in modern data protection strategies, allowing organizations to maintain multiple versions of their data and facilitating efficient management and retrieval of backup data. As data grows more complex and the demands for recovery speed and accuracy increase, versioning and backup catalogs become indispensable for ensuring data integrity and minimizing downtime during recovery. These techniques not only support effective data protection but also provide the flexibility to manage and restore data at different points in time, addressing a range of recovery scenarios from minor file restoration to large-scale disaster recovery.

Versioning refers to the practice of keeping multiple versions of the same data or files over time. This is particularly important in environments where data changes frequently, such as in collaborative workspaces, databases, or content management systems. By preserving previous versions of files or datasets, versioning provides a historical record of changes, enabling organizations to revert to earlier versions in case of errors, data corruption, or accidental deletions. For instance, if a document is accidentally overwritten with an incorrect version, or if a critical file becomes corrupted, versioning allows the restoration of the previous, uncorrupted version of the file without requiring a full restore from a backup. This level of flexibility is essential for businesses that rely on the integrity of their data and need to be able to quickly recover from mistakes or system failures.

The use of versioning can be particularly beneficial in managing backup storage efficiently. Rather than taking full backups of entire systems every time a change occurs, versioning allows incremental updates to be recorded, storing only the changes made since the last backup. This approach reduces the amount of data that needs to be backed up, saving both storage space and backup time. For example, instead of keeping multiple copies of a large file, a system using versioning will store the file with a unique identifier for each version, along with a record of the changes made. This allows for efficient storage and quick access to any previous version of the file without the need to restore the entire system from scratch. In environments where data is continuously evolving, such as databases or virtualized systems, versioning can dramatically improve the speed and efficiency of backups.

Backup catalogs, on the other hand, serve as a comprehensive inventory or index of all backups made within a given system. A backup catalog records details about each backup, including the date and time of the backup, the files or systems included, the backup type (full, incremental, differential), and the location where the backup is stored. The catalog acts as a map to the backup data, enabling administrators to quickly locate and restore specific files or system states without having to sift through an entire backup set manually. In a large-scale environment where thousands of files or systems need to be backed up and restored, a backup catalog is essential for organizing and managing the backup data efficiently.

The primary role of a backup catalog is to enable fast and accurate restores. Without a catalog, restoring a specific file from a backup could be a time-consuming process, as administrators would need to manually search through backups to find the correct version. A backup catalog streamlines this process by providing a clear record of all backup versions, making it easy to identify the right backup set for restoration. For example, if an administrator needs to restore a specific file from a backup taken three months ago, the catalog will immediately point to the relevant backup, saving significant time compared to manually searching through multiple backup media. This ability to quickly locate and restore specific files or datasets is crucial in environments where rapid recovery is essential for business operations.

Backup catalogs also help with maintaining consistency and ensuring the integrity of backup data. By tracking the status and details of each backup, catalogs can alert administrators to issues such as failed backups, incomplete backups, or missing data. This proactive approach helps prevent data loss by ensuring that backups are regularly checked and verified. In the event of a failure or corruption during the backup process, the catalog can be used to identify which parts of the data were affected, allowing for targeted recovery efforts that minimize the impact on the overall system. Moreover, backup catalogs provide a valuable audit trail, enabling organizations to demonstrate compliance with data retention policies and regulatory requirements. The catalog records all backup operations, including dates, times, and changes to the backup set, which can be essential for compliance audits.

Versioning and backup catalogs are also integral components of effective backup retention policies. Retention policies determine how long backup data is kept before it is deleted, archived, or overwritten.

Versioning allows for granular control over retention, as previous versions of data can be preserved for a defined period while older or obsolete versions are purged to free up storage space. Backup catalogs provide the necessary context to enforce these policies, as they track the age of backups and help ensure that outdated versions of data are removed according to the retention schedule. For instance, a catalog can automatically flag backups that are older than a certain retention period and either archive or delete them, ensuring that storage resources are managed efficiently without compromising data protection.

In addition to supporting retention policies, versioning and backup catalogs provide the ability to recover data at specific points in time. This is particularly valuable in environments that require point-in-time recovery, such as database systems or transactional applications. Versioning enables the restoration of data to an exact state from a previous point, while backup catalogs ensure that the appropriate backup version is selected for restoration. In environments where data changes frequently, such as in e-commerce platforms or financial institutions, having the ability to restore data to a specific time is crucial for preventing data loss or corruption caused by system failures or cyberattacks.

The implementation of versioning and backup catalogs requires thoughtful planning and the right tools to ensure that they are integrated effectively into the organization's backup strategy. Many modern backup solutions offer built-in support for versioning and backup cataloging, but organizations may also use third-party tools to extend the capabilities of their backup systems. It is important to regularly update and maintain both versioning systems and catalogs to ensure that they remain accurate and reflective of the organization's backup data. Additionally, organizations must ensure that their backup catalogs are securely stored and protected from unauthorized access, as they contain critical information about the organization's data and recovery points.

Using versioning and backup catalogs is an effective way to enhance backup strategies by providing a structured and organized approach to managing data backups. Versioning ensures that multiple iterations of data are retained, offering the flexibility to recover from previous versions in case of accidental changes or corruption. Backup catalogs streamline the recovery process by tracking the details of every backup, allowing administrators to quickly locate and restore data. These tools work together to improve data integrity, reduce recovery time, and enhance the efficiency of backup systems. As organizations continue to face growing data volumes and increasing recovery expectations, versioning and backup catalogs will remain essential components of comprehensive data protection strategies.

Handling Large-Scale Filesystem Backups

Handling large-scale filesystem backups requires a strategic approach that addresses the challenges of scalability, efficiency, and reliability. As data volumes continue to grow exponentially, organizations need to adopt backup solutions that can effectively manage the complexity of large datasets without compromising the performance of their systems or introducing excessive downtime. A comprehensive strategy for large-scale backups involves not only selecting the right backup tools and storage solutions but also implementing optimized processes that ensure data integrity and availability while minimizing backup windows and resource usage. The process of managing large-scale backups can be daunting, but with the right planning and best practices in place, it is possible to achieve reliable and efficient data protection at scale.

One of the primary challenges of handling large-scale filesystem backups is the sheer volume of data that needs to be backed up. For organizations with vast amounts of data, traditional backup methods, such as full backups, can be time-consuming and resource-intensive. Full backups, which copy all the data from a filesystem or volume, may take hours or even days to complete, depending on the size of the dataset and the performance of the backup infrastructure. To mitigate this issue, many large-scale backup solutions rely on incremental or differential backups, which only capture changes made since the last full backup or the last incremental backup. These methods reduce the amount of data that needs to be backed up, speeding up the backup process and minimizing the impact on system performance. However, incremental and differential backups require a more complex restoration process, as all the relevant backups must be applied in sequence to restore the system to a specific point in time. Despite this complexity, incremental and differential backups offer significant advantages in terms of reducing backup time and storage requirements.

In addition to selecting the right backup method, managing large-scale backups requires choosing an appropriate backup infrastructure. The storage solutions used for large-scale backups must be capable of handling high volumes of data efficiently and securely. Local storage solutions, such as network-attached storage (NAS) or direct-attached storage (DAS), are often used for backing up large datasets, as they offer fast read and write speeds and are relatively simple to manage. However, local storage may not provide sufficient scalability or redundancy for larger environments, especially if the data needs to be backed up across multiple locations or stored off-site for disaster recovery. Cloud storage solutions, on the other hand, offer greater scalability and flexibility, allowing organizations to store vast amounts of data without the need for significant capital investment in physical infrastructure. Cloud-based backup solutions can be particularly beneficial for large-scale backups, as they provide virtually unlimited storage capacity and enable off-site data protection, which is critical for disaster recovery scenarios. However, cloud backups often introduce new considerations, such as bandwidth limitations and data transfer costs, which must be carefully managed to ensure the backup process remains efficient.

Another critical factor in handling large-scale backups is network bandwidth. Large volumes of data require significant network resources to transfer, and network congestion can lead to slow backup times and increased backup windows. When performing backups across a network, it is essential to optimize the bandwidth usage to ensure that backup operations do not interfere with other critical network activities, such as production traffic or application performance. Many large-scale backup solutions offer features such as bandwidth throttling, which allows administrators to control the amount of network bandwidth allocated to backup tasks. This ensures that backup operations do not consume excessive network resources during peak usage hours, reducing the impact on overall system performance. Additionally, techniques such as data compression and deduplication can be employed to minimize the amount of data that needs to be transferred over the network, further optimizing the backup process.

Deduplication is particularly useful in large-scale backup environments, as it eliminates redundant data across multiple backup sets. In many cases, large datasets contain duplicate files or data blocks that do not need to be backed up multiple times. Deduplication ensures that only unique data is stored, reducing the overall storage requirements and improving backup efficiency. Many modern backup solutions incorporate deduplication technology, either at the source or target level, to optimize backup storage and speed up the backup process. Source-side deduplication eliminates redundant data before it is transferred over the network, while target-side deduplication removes duplicates after the data has been received. Both methods offer substantial benefits in terms of reducing the amount of storage required for backups and improving the overall performance of large-scale backup operations.

Managing backup schedules is another important aspect of handling large-scale filesystem backups. With large volumes of data, backup windows must be carefully planned to ensure that backups are completed in a timely manner without disrupting critical business operations. Running backups during peak business hours can negatively impact system performance, leading to slowdowns and reduced productivity. To minimize this impact, many organizations schedule backups to run during off-peak hours, such as overnight or on weekends, when system demand is lower. In some cases, organizations may also adopt continuous or near-continuous backup strategies, where data is backed up in smaller, incremental chunks throughout the day. This allows for more frequent backups without causing significant performance degradation. However, continuous backups require robust infrastructure and efficient backup solutions to ensure that data is consistently protected without overwhelming network or storage resources.

One of the key considerations in handling large-scale backups is ensuring data integrity and recoverability. As the size and complexity of backup datasets grow, the risk of errors or corruption increases. It is essential to implement regular integrity checks to verify that backup data is complete, uncorrupted, and ready for restoration. Many modern backup solutions offer built-in verification features that perform checksum or hash-based checks on backup data, ensuring that the backed-up data matches the original source. These verification checks should be performed regularly to identify any issues early on, allowing administrators to correct any problems before they affect the restore process. Additionally, performing test restores is essential for ensuring that backup data can be recovered accurately and efficiently. In a large-scale environment, testing restores of both full systems and individual files ensures that the backup infrastructure is functioning as expected and that the data can be restored when needed.

Finally, monitoring and reporting are critical components of managing large-scale filesystem backups. Monitoring tools provide real-time insights into the status and performance of backup jobs, allowing administrators to track progress, identify failures, and resolve issues before they impact data protection efforts. Backup reporting tools generate detailed logs and reports that track backup success rates, storage usage, and any errors encountered during the backup process. These reports help administrators maintain visibility over large-scale backup operations and ensure that the backup infrastructure remains reliable and effective. Regular monitoring and reporting also help with compliance, as they provide a record of backup activities and ensure that backup policies are being followed consistently.

Handling large-scale filesystem backups involves addressing a variety of challenges, from optimizing backup methods and storage infrastructure to ensuring data integrity and minimizing network impact. By implementing efficient backup strategies, leveraging technologies such as deduplication and compression, and carefully managing backup schedules and resources, organizations can ensure that their large-scale backup operations are both effective and reliable. With the growing importance of data protection and disaster recovery, adopting best practices for handling large-scale backups is essential for safeguarding critical data and ensuring business continuity.

Backup Strategies for Virtualized Environments

As virtualization technology becomes an integral part of modern IT infrastructures, it presents unique challenges and opportunities for backup strategies. Virtualized environments, which often involve the use of hypervisors such as VMware, Hyper-V, or KVM to manage virtual machines (VMs), introduce complexities in data protection due to the nature of the virtualization layer. Unlike traditional physical environments, where backup processes focus on individual machines and their data, virtualized environments require strategies that can handle multiple VMs running on a single physical host, often with different configurations and workloads. Effectively protecting virtualized environments requires a shift in backup methods, a deeper understanding of the virtualization platform, and the deployment of appropriate tools to ensure data availability and recoverability.

The first step in developing a backup strategy for virtualized environments is understanding the key differences between traditional physical servers and virtual machines. A virtual machine is essentially a software emulation of a physical computer, running its own operating system and applications but sharing the underlying hardware resources with other VMs on the same host. This abstraction layer provides flexibility in resource allocation, scaling, and management but also introduces challenges in ensuring that backup processes are efficient and do not interfere with VM performance. Additionally, virtualized environments can have a high density of VMs running on a single physical host, which increases the complexity of managing backups for each virtual machine and their associated data.

In virtualized environments, one of the primary methods for backing up data is to use image-based backups. Image-based backups capture an entire virtual machine, including the operating system, applications, configurations, and data, in a single backup file. This type of backup is particularly effective for virtualized environments because it ensures that the entire VM can be restored to its previous state with minimal effort, making it easier to recover from system failures, corruption, or accidental deletions. Image-based backups can be taken at the VM level or the hypervisor level, allowing for flexibility in how data is protected and restored. Hypervisor-level backups can provide additional benefits, such as the ability to back up multiple VMs simultaneously or to restore VMs across different physical hosts.

One of the advantages of image-based backups in virtualized environments is that they allow for faster and more efficient recovery. Restoring an entire virtual machine from an image backup is typically quicker than restoring individual files or directories, as it eliminates the need for separate operating system, application, and data restores. This fast recovery process is essential in virtualized environments, where minimizing downtime is a priority. Moreover, with image-based backups, administrators can restore a VM to a specific point in time, which is useful for recovering from issues like application failures or data corruption.

However, while image-based backups offer speed and simplicity, they also come with certain challenges. For instance, the large size of image backups can lead to storage inefficiencies, especially when multiple VMs are backed up on a regular basis. Storing image backups for a high number of VMs can quickly consume vast amounts of storage space, especially in environments with many virtualized workloads. To address this issue, organizations often use deduplication technologies that eliminate redundant data across backups, reducing the overall storage requirements. Deduplication ensures that only unique data is stored, making it more efficient and cost-effective to back up large numbers of VMs.

Another challenge with image-based backups is the potential for backup windows to extend significantly as the number of virtual machines grows. To mitigate this, organizations often rely on incremental and differential backups, which only capture changes made since the last full backup. This method reduces the backup time and storage requirements, making it more feasible to back up a large number of VMs frequently. Incremental and differential backups, however, require careful management, as restoring from them can be more complex than performing a full image restore. In cases where a specific VM must be restored to a particular point in time, administrators must ensure that all relevant incremental or differential backups are available and intact to restore the system fully.

Virtual machine snapshots are another important tool for backup strategies in virtualized environments. Snapshots capture the state of a VM at a particular point in time and can be used to restore the VM to that state in the event of a failure. Snapshots are often used in conjunction with regular backup processes to create a consistent backup while the VM is running. However, snapshots should not be used as a long-term backup solution, as they can negatively impact the performance of the VM if left in place for extended periods. Snapshots should be taken periodically and then backed up or merged into regular backup sets to ensure that data is adequately protected.

One of the significant advantages of backing up virtualized environments is the ability to use tools and features provided by the hypervisor to streamline backup processes. Many hypervisors, such as VMware vSphere or Microsoft Hyper-V, offer integrated backup solutions that can back up VMs efficiently and with minimal disruption to the virtualized infrastructure. These solutions allow for features like backup automation, scheduling, and integration with storage devices, simplifying the management of backups. For example, VMware vSphere provides the VMware Data Protection (VDP) feature, which allows administrators to back up entire virtual machines, perform restores, and manage backup schedules through a central interface. Hyper-V offers similar features with its built-in Windows Server Backup tool, which can be used for backing up both individual VMs and entire virtualized environments.

Backup strategies for virtualized environments should also include offsite or cloud backups to ensure that data is protected from local disasters, such as fires, floods, or thefts. Cloud backups provide a scalable, offsite solution for storing VM backups and ensure that data is available for recovery even if the primary data center is compromised. Cloud backup services typically offer automated backup solutions that can be easily integrated with existing virtualized environments, reducing the complexity of managing offsite backups. Cloud-based solutions also offer flexible storage options, allowing organizations to scale their backup storage as needed and reducing the need for expensive on-premises hardware. However, using cloud backups introduces considerations around bandwidth usage, security, and recovery time, which must be addressed during the planning phase.

To ensure that backup strategies in virtualized environments are effective, it is essential to regularly test and validate backups. Testing ensures that data can be restored as expected and that the backup strategy is meeting recovery objectives. Regular restore tests should be performed to ensure that VMs can be recovered quickly and accurately in the event of a failure. Testing also helps identify any gaps in the backup process, such as missed virtual machines, outdated snapshots, or corrupted backup files. By regularly testing backups and restoring VMs to a separate test environment, organizations can ensure that their backup processes are reliable and capable of supporting business continuity during a disaster.

Ultimately, backup strategies for virtualized environments must be tailored to the specific needs of the organization. Virtualization presents unique opportunities for optimizing backup processes and improving recovery times, but it also introduces challenges that require careful planning and management. By utilizing image-based backups, snapshots, and integrated hypervisor tools, organizations can effectively back up and protect their virtualized workloads. Regular testing, offsite backups, and the use of deduplication technologies further enhance the effectiveness of virtualized backup strategies, ensuring that data can be restored quickly and reliably when required. As virtualized environments continue to evolve, so too must the strategies for managing and protecting them, ensuring that backup systems remain effective in safeguarding critical business data.

Best Practices for Remote and Offsite Backups

Remote and offsite backups are essential components of a robust data protection strategy. By storing copies of data in locations separate from the primary site, organizations can safeguard against local disasters such as fires, floods, theft, or hardware failure. While on-site backups are critical for quick recovery in everyday situations, remote and offsite backups provide a critical layer of protection, ensuring data availability even in the most catastrophic scenarios. The strategy for implementing remote and offsite backups must be carefully designed to balance security, reliability, efficiency, and cost. Best practices for remote and offsite backups help ensure that data is not only protected but can also be restored quickly and accurately in the event of a disaster.

One of the key considerations when implementing remote and offsite backups is selecting the right location for storing backup data. The location of offsite backups must be carefully chosen to ensure it is safe from the same risks that affect the primary data center. For example, a backup stored in the same physical location as the main data center could be compromised by a local disaster, such as a fire or flood. Offsite storage should be located in a geographically separate area, ideally in a different city or region, to mitigate the risk of simultaneous destruction of both the primary site and the backup. This geographic separation ensures that the backup data is not vulnerable to the same regional threats. Many organizations also consider cloud-based storage solutions as part of their offsite backup strategy, as cloud providers offer geographically redundant data centers that can further protect backup data.

In addition to the physical location of offsite backups, organizations must ensure that the transfer of backup data to remote locations is secure. Data in transit can be intercepted or tampered with, which is why encryption is a critical consideration when performing remote backups. Encrypting backup data during transmission ensures that even if the data is intercepted, it remains unreadable to unauthorized parties. Many backup solutions incorporate end-to-end encryption, which encrypts data before it is transmitted over the network and keeps it encrypted until it is restored. The encryption should be strong, with modern standards such as AES-256, to ensure the security of sensitive information. Along with encryption, secure transmission protocols like SSL/TLS or VPNs (Virtual Private Networks) should be used to further protect data as it travels between the primary site and the offsite backup location.

Bandwidth limitations are another important consideration for remote and offsite backups. Backing up large volumes of data across a network can consume significant bandwidth, especially when dealing with high-frequency backups or large datasets. To mitigate the impact of network congestion, backup processes should be scheduled to run during off-peak hours, such as during the night or weekends, when network usage is low. Additionally, many remote backup solutions support compression and deduplication technologies, which reduce the amount of data that needs to be transmitted. Data compression shrinks backup files before they are sent, and deduplication eliminates redundant data, ensuring that only unique information is transferred. These technologies optimize bandwidth usage, reducing the strain on the network and improving the overall efficiency of remote backups.

For businesses using cloud-based offsite backups, understanding the service-level agreements (SLAs) and the associated costs is crucial. Cloud providers typically offer different storage tiers, such as hot, warm, and cold storage, which vary in terms of access speed, cost, and durability. Hot storage offers immediate access to backup data, making it ideal for frequent or emergency restores, but it tends to be more expensive. Cold storage, on the other hand, is more cost-effective for data that is rarely accessed but still needs to be retained for compliance or archival purposes. Organizations must choose the appropriate storage tier based on their recovery objectives, access needs, and budget. Additionally, while cloud-based storage offers scalability and flexibility, it is important to ensure that the cloud provider has strong security protocols in place and that data redundancy and backup verification measures are being followed.

Retaining remote and offsite backup data for the appropriate period is another key practice. Retention policies define how long backup data should be stored before being deleted, archived, or overwritten. These policies should be tailored to the organization's regulatory requirements, business needs, and available storage capacity. For example, some industries, such as healthcare and finance, require that backup data be kept for several years to comply with regulatory standards. On the other hand, for some less regulated industries, a shorter retention period may suffice. Backup retention policies should ensure that old and unnecessary backups are removed or archived properly to free up space for new backups. Regularly reviewing and adjusting retention policies ensures that storage resources are being used efficiently and that compliance requirements are consistently met.

Testing remote and offsite backups is essential for ensuring that data can be restored when needed. Many organizations make the mistake of assuming that their backups will work without regularly testing them, but the only way to confirm that a backup is usable is by restoring data from it. Regularly testing backups ensures that they are complete, accessible, and free of corruption. Restore tests should be performed periodically, and the restore process should be documented to ensure that it can be completed smoothly in the event of a real disaster. Testing should also include recovery from both full and incremental backups to ensure that the entire backup chain is functional. In a large-scale environment, testing the restoration of individual files and entire systems across different recovery points helps ensure that all backup data is recoverable.

Another important practice for managing remote and offsite backups is the use of automation. Automating backup schedules, monitoring, and reporting ensures that backups are performed consistently and reduces the risk of human error. Backup automation can include scheduling backups to occur at specific intervals, verifying backup completion, and generating alerts if a backup fails. Automation also helps ensure that backups are performed during off-peak hours, minimizing the impact on network performance. By automating the backup process, organizations can ensure that remote and offsite backups are executed regularly and according to the defined backup strategy, without requiring constant manual intervention.

Monitoring remote and offsite backups is also critical for identifying potential issues before they result in data loss. Monitoring tools track the status of backups, alert administrators about any failures or inconsistencies, and provide reports on backup performance. These tools should be integrated into the organization's broader IT monitoring system, providing a centralized view of all backup activities. Real-time monitoring allows administrators to detect problems, such as slow backup speeds, failed transfers, or storage capacity issues, and take corrective action quickly. Proactive monitoring ensures that backup processes are working as expected, and that any issues are resolved before they can jeopardize the safety of backup data.

Finally, organizations should consider integrating offsite backups into their broader disaster recovery and business continuity plans. Remote backups are an essential part of disaster recovery strategies, as they provide a reliable way to restore data in the event of a catastrophic failure at the primary site. Offsite backups, particularly cloud-based solutions, can provide not only data protection but also disaster recovery capabilities, allowing for rapid recovery of critical systems and applications. A well-defined disaster recovery plan that includes remote and offsite backups helps ensure that the organization can continue operations with minimal disruption, even in the face of unforeseen events.

By following best practices for remote and offsite backups, organizations can ensure that their data is well protected from local disasters and that it is recoverable when needed. A well-structured offsite backup strategy improves data availability, reduces the risk of data loss, and supports compliance with regulatory requirements. These practices ensure that backup systems are both reliable and efficient, providing organizations with the confidence that their critical data is always safe, regardless of the circumstances.

Legal and Compliance Considerations in Backup Strategies

Legal and compliance considerations are critical components of any backup strategy, as businesses must ensure that their data protection practices align with various laws and regulations that govern data privacy, retention, and security. These regulations can vary widely across industries and regions, and non-compliance can result in severe penalties, legal liabilities, and damage to a company's reputation. As organizations face increasing scrutiny over their data management practices, having a robust backup strategy that considers legal and compliance requirements is essential for safeguarding sensitive information and avoiding legal risks.

One of the primary concerns when developing a backup strategy is understanding the legal requirements related to data retention. Many industries, including healthcare, finance, and government, are subject to specific regulations that dictate how long certain types of data must be retained. For example, healthcare organizations in the United States must comply with the Health Insurance Portability and Accountability Act (HIPAA), which requires the retention of patient records for a minimum of six years. Similarly, financial institutions must adhere to the Sarbanes-Oxley Act (SOX), which mandates the retention of certain financial records for a defined period to ensure transparency and accountability. Understanding these retention requirements is essential when designing backup strategies to ensure that data is not prematurely deleted or retained for longer than required.

Organizations must also be aware of the requirements for securely storing and protecting backup data. Data security is a critical aspect of compliance, especially when handling sensitive or personally identifiable information (PII). Regulations such as the General Data Protection Regulation (GDPR) in the European Union, the California Consumer Privacy Act (CCPA), and HIPAA impose strict guidelines on how organizations must protect customer and employee data. These regulations often require that data be encrypted both at rest and in transit, ensuring that unauthorized individuals cannot access the data, whether it is stored on physical backup devices or transmitted to offsite locations. Encryption is an essential component of any backup strategy, and organizations must ensure that they implement strong encryption standards to protect sensitive data, especially when using remote or cloud-based storage.

Compliance also involves maintaining proper access controls over backup data. Legal and regulatory frameworks often require that only authorized personnel have access to backup data, and organizations must implement access control mechanisms to enforce this. Role-based access control (RBAC) and multi-factor authentication (MFA) are widely used to restrict access to backup systems and data. RBAC allows organizations to grant access based on the user's role within the organization, ensuring that only those with a legitimate need can access or restore backup data. MFA adds an extra layer of security by requiring users to provide multiple forms of identification before they can access backup data, further protecting against unauthorized access.

Another important legal consideration in backup strategies is data residency. Many countries have laws that regulate where data can be stored, especially for organizations operating in multiple jurisdictions.

Data residency laws require that certain types of data, particularly personal data, be stored within the borders of a specific country or region. For example, the GDPR imposes restrictions on transferring personal data outside the European Union, and organizations must ensure that any cross-border data transfers comply with the regulation's provisions. This has significant implications for organizations that rely on cloud services or offsite backup solutions, as they must ensure that their data storage providers comply with data residency requirements. Failure to comply with these laws can result in substantial fines and penalties, making it critical for organizations to carefully vet their backup and cloud service providers.

Backup strategies must also account for the proper management and disposal of backup data. When data is no longer needed or has reached the end of its retention period, organizations must ensure that it is securely deleted or destroyed. Data deletion practices are subject to regulations that require organizations to eliminate sensitive data in a way that ensures it cannot be recovered or reconstructed. For example, the GDPR mandates that personal data be erased when it is no longer necessary for the purposes for which it was collected, and similar requirements exist in other data privacy laws. Secure data destruction practices, such as data wiping or physical destruction of storage devices, are essential to ensure compliance with these regulations. Backup data that is not properly destroyed can be a significant security and legal risk, as unauthorized individuals may attempt to recover it for malicious purposes.

Auditing and reporting are also critical aspects of ensuring compliance in backup strategies. Many legal and regulatory frameworks require organizations to maintain records of their backup processes, including details on the types of data backed up, the frequency of backups, and the retention period for each dataset. These records can be used in audits to demonstrate compliance with data protection laws. Backup systems should have built-in logging and reporting capabilities that track backup activities and provide detailed reports on the success or failure of backup jobs, access to backup data, and any issues encountered during the backup process. These logs can be crucial for providing evidence in case of a data breach or regulatory investigation and for ensuring that backup processes are operating in accordance with organizational policies and legal requirements.

Organizations that operate in multiple industries or regions must also be aware of the complexity of managing compliance across different regulatory frameworks. Different laws may impose conflicting requirements, such as differing data retention periods or varying levels of access control. In these cases, it is essential for organizations to adopt a flexible and adaptable backup strategy that can accommodate the most stringent requirements of all relevant regulations. This may involve setting up separate backup processes or storage solutions for different types of data, ensuring that compliance is maintained without violating other legal obligations. Organizations may also consider working with legal and compliance experts to navigate the complexities of these regulations and ensure that their backup strategies are fully aligned with the law.

In addition to meeting specific legal and regulatory requirements, organizations must also consider industry best practices when developing their backup strategies. Following industry standards, such as the NIST Cybersecurity Framework or ISO 27001, helps ensure that backup strategies align with recognized security and data protection practices. These standards provide guidance on everything from backup frequency and encryption to access controls and audit logging. Adhering to these best practices can help organizations not only meet legal and compliance requirements but also establish a comprehensive data protection strategy that mitigates risks and enhances overall security.

Legal and compliance considerations are foundational to the design and implementation of effective backup strategies. By understanding and addressing the complex regulatory landscape, organizations can ensure that their backup systems are compliant with data protection laws and capable of safeguarding sensitive information. This includes implementing strong encryption, access controls, and data retention policies while also ensuring secure data destruction and thorough audit practices. As legal requirements evolve, organizations must continually reassess their backup strategies to ensure ongoing compliance and avoid potential legal consequences. By integrating legal and compliance considerations into their backup practices, organizations can strengthen their data protection capabilities and reduce their exposure to legal risks.

Data Deduplication in Backup Systems

Data deduplication is a critical technique used in backup systems to optimize storage efficiency and reduce the amount of redundant data stored across backup sets. As the volume of data continues to grow exponentially, organizations must find ways to manage and store backup data more effectively, ensuring that they can protect critical information without incurring prohibitive storage costs. Deduplication addresses this challenge by identifying and eliminating duplicate data, ensuring that only unique information is stored, which significantly reduces the amount of storage required. This technique can be applied to both local and remote backup systems, whether using traditional disk-based storage or cloud storage solutions, and is an essential component of modern data protection strategies.

At its core, data deduplication works by scanning backup data for identical blocks or segments and replacing redundant copies with references to a single stored copy. Instead of storing every instance of a file or block of data, deduplication ensures that only one copy of each unique piece of data is saved. When a new backup is performed, the system checks whether the data being backed up already exists in the backup repository. If it does, the system stores a reference to the existing data rather than duplicating it. This process reduces the overall size of the backup, saving significant amounts of storage space and improving backup performance.

One of the most significant advantages of data deduplication is the reduction in storage requirements. Backups often contain large amounts of redundant data, particularly in environments where many systems share common files or datasets. For example, in virtualized environments, multiple virtual machines may share the same operating system files or applications. Without deduplication, each virtual machine's backup would store duplicate copies of these shared files, leading to unnecessary consumption of storage space. Deduplication eliminates this redundancy by ensuring that only one copy of the shared data is stored, regardless of how many virtual machines reference it. This results in a more efficient use of storage resources and can help organizations manage the growing demands of data protection.

Deduplication is particularly effective in scenarios where data changes incrementally over time, such as in incremental backups. With traditional incremental backups, only the data that has changed since the last full backup is saved, which reduces the amount of data being backed up. However, even in incremental backups, there can still be significant redundancy, especially when large files are being modified frequently. Deduplication helps further reduce this redundancy by identifying repeating data blocks within the changed files and eliminating duplicates before they are saved. This ensures that only new or modified data is stored, optimizing the backup process and reducing the amount of storage needed.

There are two main types of data deduplication: file-level and block-level. File-level deduplication identifies and eliminates duplicate files across backups. When a file is backed up, the system checks whether it already exists in the backup storage. If it does, the system replaces the duplicate file with a reference to the existing copy. While file-level deduplication is effective for eliminating duplicate files, it does not provide the same level of granularity as block-level deduplication. Block-level deduplication, on the other hand, divides files into smaller chunks or blocks and eliminates duplicates at the block level. This type of deduplication is more efficient in environments with high levels of file changes or where large files are frequently modified. Block-level deduplication ensures that only the unique blocks of data are stored, even if the file itself is modified multiple times.

The implementation of data deduplication can take place at either the source or the target of the backup process. Source-side deduplication occurs before the data is transmitted to the backup storage, reducing the amount of data sent over the network. This is particularly useful in remote backup environments or when backing up large datasets to the cloud, as it minimizes bandwidth usage and speeds up the backup process. By eliminating duplicates at the source, only unique data is transmitted to the storage location, reducing both the time required for the backup and the storage needed to hold the backup data. Target-side deduplication, on the other hand, occurs after the data has been transmitted to the storage system. This approach is typically used in disk-based backup solutions and reduces storage requirements by deduplicating data after it has been received. While target-side deduplication requires more storage capacity and processing power at the backup storage site, it allows for more flexibility and can be easier to manage in environments with high data throughput.

While deduplication offers significant storage savings and performance improvements, it is important to understand its impact on backup and recovery processes. Deduplication can reduce the size of backup files, which in turn reduces the amount of data that needs to be transferred, stored, and managed. However, this reduction in data volume can sometimes introduce complexity when it comes to restoring data. Since deduplication involves replacing redundant data with references to a single copy, restoring a backup may require the system to access and reassemble multiple data blocks from different parts of the backup repository. This process can increase the time required for data restoration, particularly in environments with a high level of deduplication or when restoring from remote locations. As a result, organizations must carefully consider their recovery time objectives (RTOs) and ensure that the deduplication process does not interfere with the speed of recovery during a disaster or system failure.

Another consideration when using deduplication is the impact on backup performance, particularly in environments with large datasets or complex data structures. While deduplication reduces the amount of data to be stored, it can require additional processing power to identify and eliminate redundant data. This may cause delays during the backup process, particularly if the backup system is not equipped with sufficient resources to handle the deduplication process efficiently. Organizations need to ensure that their backup infrastructure is capable of handling the increased processing requirements of deduplication without compromising performance or introducing bottlenecks. In some cases, dedicated hardware accelerators or appliances may be required to optimize deduplication performance.

Data deduplication also plays a critical role in compliance and data retention strategies. In industries with stringent regulatory requirements, such as healthcare or finance, organizations must retain backup data for long periods of time while ensuring that it remains secure and easily retrievable. Deduplication helps meet these retention requirements by minimizing the amount of data stored, making it easier to manage long-term backups and reducing the cost of storage. By reducing storage costs, organizations can retain more backup data without exceeding their storage budgets, while still meeting compliance requirements. Deduplication also helps ensure that only the necessary data is stored, which can be important for compliance with data privacy regulations that require the deletion or anonymization of unnecessary or outdated data.

Data deduplication is an indispensable technology in modern backup systems, offering substantial benefits in terms of storage efficiency, backup speed, and cost savings. Whether applied at the file or block level, deduplication optimizes backup processes by eliminating redundant data, ensuring that only unique information is stored. This technique is particularly effective in environments where data changes frequently or where large datasets need to be backed up regularly. However, it is important for organizations to carefully consider the impact of deduplication on backup and recovery times, as well as the processing resources required to perform the deduplication process efficiently. With careful planning and the right infrastructure, deduplication can play a vital role in improving the overall efficiency and effectiveness of backup strategies, helping organizations manage their data protection needs while minimizing costs.

Backup and Filesystem Management for Cloud Environments

As organizations continue to migrate their operations to the cloud, managing backups and filesystems in cloud environments has become a crucial component of overall data protection strategies. The flexibility, scalability, and cost-effectiveness of cloud storage solutions have transformed how businesses approach data backup, offering the ability to store vast amounts of data off-site while ensuring accessibility and security. However, with these advantages come unique challenges, including managing the complexities of cloud-based filesystems, ensuring that data is backed up efficiently, and adhering to compliance regulations. A well-designed backup and filesystem management strategy in the cloud is essential to ensure data integrity, availability, and security while mitigating the risks associated with cloud storage.

In cloud environments, backup strategies must be adapted to account for the distributed and often complex nature of cloud infrastructure. Unlike traditional on-premises backups, which typically involve backing up data to local storage devices, cloud-based backups involve transferring data over the internet to remote data centers managed by cloud service providers. These data centers are often located in multiple geographic regions, offering redundancy and protection against localized disasters. When designing a backup strategy for cloud environments, it is essential to choose the appropriate cloud service model, whether it is Infrastructure as a Service (IaaS), Platform as a Service (PaaS), or Software as a Service (SaaS), as each model offers different levels of control and management over data.

For organizations using IaaS, where virtual machines (VMs) and storage resources are provided as a service, backup strategies typically involve creating snapshots of VMs and backing up data to cloud storage solutions. Snapshots are an efficient way to create point-in-time copies of entire systems, allowing administrators to restore VMs quickly in the event of a failure. These snapshots can be automated and scheduled to ensure that VMs are consistently backed up without requiring manual intervention. Cloud storage solutions, such as Amazon S3 or Azure Blob Storage, can be used to store backup data, offering durability, scalability, and security. The cloud service provider manages the underlying storage infrastructure, ensuring that the data is replicated across multiple regions to provide high availability and protection against data loss.

One of the key advantages of cloud storage for backups is its scalability. Cloud providers offer flexible storage options that can grow or shrink based on the organization's needs, allowing businesses to pay only for the storage they actually use. This scalability is particularly beneficial for organizations with fluctuating backup requirements, as they can easily adjust their storage capacity as needed. Cloud storage also eliminates the need for organizations to maintain on-site backup infrastructure, reducing costs associated with hardware, power, and maintenance. However, scalability also introduces challenges related to data transfer and bandwidth. Uploading large volumes of data to the cloud can consume significant bandwidth, especially for organizations with limited internet connections. To mitigate these challenges, organizations may need to implement techniques such as compression and deduplication to reduce the amount of data that needs to be transferred.

Another important consideration in cloud backup and filesystem management is security. Cloud providers implement a variety of security measures to protect data at rest and in transit, such as encryption and access control mechanisms. However, it is still the organization's responsibility to ensure that data is securely encrypted before being transferred to the cloud. Encryption ensures that even if the backup data is intercepted during transfer, it remains unreadable to unauthorized individuals. Additionally, organizations should ensure that proper access controls are in place to restrict who can access or modify backup data. Multi-factor authentication (MFA) should be used to provide an additional layer of security, ensuring that only authorized personnel can access backup systems and restore data.

Cloud providers typically offer built-in tools for backup and filesystem management, but organizations may also choose to implement third-party backup solutions to better meet their specific needs. These solutions can provide more granular control over backup schedules, retention policies, and data recovery processes. Many third-party solutions integrate directly with cloud storage services, enabling seamless backup and recovery processes across hybrid cloud environments. These solutions often offer features such as incremental backups, which only back up changes made since the last backup, and continuous data protection, which ensures that data is backed up in real-time as changes occur. These features reduce the amount of data that needs to be transferred and stored, optimizing bandwidth and storage efficiency.

Data retention is another critical aspect of backup and filesystem management in cloud environments. Cloud storage providers typically offer different storage tiers with varying levels of access speed and cost. For example, Amazon S3 provides options such as Standard Storage for frequently accessed data, Glacier for archival data, and Intelligent-Tiering for automatically moving data between storage classes based on access patterns. Organizations must define retention policies that specify how long backup data should be kept and when it should be archived or deleted. Cloud backup solutions can automate retention management, ensuring that older backups are moved to lower-cost storage tiers or deleted when they are no longer needed. Proper retention policies help organizations manage storage costs and ensure compliance with regulatory requirements.

The complexity of managing large volumes of backup data in the cloud also requires effective monitoring and reporting. Cloud backup systems should be monitored regularly to ensure that backups are completing successfully and that data is being stored securely. Monitoring tools can provide real-time alerts in the event of a backup failure, network issues, or other problems, allowing administrators to address issues quickly before they impact business operations. Many cloud backup solutions provide dashboards and reporting tools that offer insights into backup performance, storage usage, and recovery times, helping organizations optimize their backup strategies and ensure that their data protection practices meet their recovery objectives.

Another challenge in cloud backup and filesystem management is ensuring compliance with regulatory requirements. Many industries, such as healthcare, finance, and government, have strict data protection regulations that mandate how data should be stored, backed up, and retained. For example, the Health Insurance Portability and Accountability Act (HIPAA) requires healthcare organizations to maintain secure backups of patient data, while the General Data Protection Regulation (GDPR) in the European Union imposes strict rules on data storage and access. Cloud service providers typically offer features that help organizations comply with these regulations, such as data encryption, access controls, and audit logging. However, organizations must ensure that their backup strategies align with these requirements and that they are using the appropriate cloud storage solutions to meet their compliance obligations.

Lastly, cloud backup and filesystem management must account for disaster recovery and business continuity. In the event of a major system failure, data corruption, or security breach, organizations need to be able to restore their data quickly and efficiently. Cloud backup systems often support disaster recovery by enabling organizations to restore their data to different locations or recover entire systems from backup images. This flexibility is essential for minimizing downtime and ensuring that business operations can continue uninterrupted. Many cloud providers also offer disaster recovery as a service, allowing organizations to replicate their data to multiple regions and quickly failover to a secondary site in case of a disaster.

Backup and filesystem management in cloud environments require a careful balance of security, scalability, efficiency, and compliance. By leveraging the flexibility and cost-effectiveness of cloud storage, organizations can optimize their backup strategies, ensuring that data is protected, recoverable, and compliant with industry regulations. However, as cloud-based backup solutions continue to evolve, organizations must remain vigilant in managing their data protection practices, addressing emerging challenges, and continuously improving their backup strategies to keep pace with changing technological and regulatory landscapes.

Handling Databases in Filesystem Backups

Databases are a core component of modern IT infrastructures, storing critical business data, applications, and records. As such, managing databases within filesystem backups presents a unique set of challenges. Unlike regular files, databases are dynamic, with data constantly being read, written, or updated, often in real-time. When backing up a filesystem that includes databases, it is essential to account for the transactional nature of databases and ensure that backup copies are consistent and reliable. A key aspect of successful database backup management is ensuring data integrity, minimizing downtime, and maintaining performance throughout the backup process.

The first challenge in handling databases within filesystem backups is ensuring consistency. Databases often store large amounts of transactional data that can change frequently. During a traditional filesystem backup, these changes can occur in the middle of the backup process, leading to inconsistent or corrupted backups. If a database is backed up while it is being actively written to, the resulting backup may contain partial transactions or incomplete data. This could cause issues during a restore process, making the recovery of the database inaccurate or impossible. To avoid this, specialized techniques are required to ensure that database backups capture data in a consistent state.

One of the most common approaches for achieving consistency in database backups is to use application-aware backup methods. Application-aware backups ensure that the backup process is fully integrated with the database management system (DBMS). These methods typically rely on database-specific backup tools or APIs (Application Programming Interfaces) to quiesce the database before taking a backup. Quiescing a database involves temporarily freezing database activity or pausing transactions to ensure that no data is being written while the backup is occurring. This creates a consistent snapshot of the database that can be safely backed up. Once the backup is complete, the database resumes normal operations. Many DBMSs, such as Microsoft SQL Server, Oracle, and MySQL, have built-in tools for creating application-consistent backups that integrate with backup systems to ensure data integrity.

In cases where application-aware backup tools are unavailable or unsuitable, an alternative method is to rely on database transaction logs. Most modern relational databases maintain transaction logs, which record every change made to the database. By using transaction logs, administrators can perform backups that capture changes made to the database at specific intervals, ensuring that data is always recoverable. Transaction log backups are particularly useful in large-scale environments, where full backups may be performed infrequently, but incremental changes are captured more often. By combining full database backups with transaction log backups, organizations can ensure that data can be restored to the exact point in time it was backed up, reducing the risk of data loss. However, transaction log backups require careful management to ensure that logs are properly truncated and rotated to prevent them from consuming excessive storage space.

When handling databases in filesystem backups, organizations must also consider the impact on performance. Backup operations, particularly for large databases, can place significant strain on the system. Traditional filesystem backups can cause high disk I/O, network traffic, and CPU usage, which may affect the performance of the database or the overall system. To mitigate these impacts, it is important to schedule backups during off-peak hours or periods of low system demand. Additionally, some backup systems support incremental backups or differential backups, which only back up the changes made since the last full backup. These types of backups reduce the load on the system by limiting the amount of data transferred and processed during the backup.

Another critical consideration when backing up databases is the choice of storage for the backup files. Databases can be large, and the storage requirements for a comprehensive database backup can quickly become substantial. When selecting backup storage, it is essential to choose a solution that is scalable, reliable, and secure. Cloud-based backup solutions have become increasingly popular for database backups, as they offer flexibility, scalability, and offsite storage for disaster recovery purposes. Cloud storage can also be integrated with automated backup solutions, making it easier to manage and store backups of large databases without the need for on-premises hardware. However, when using cloud-based backups, organizations must ensure that sufficient bandwidth is available to handle large data transfers, particularly for frequent backups of large databases.

For organizations with high availability or disaster recovery requirements, backup strategies should incorporate redundancy and offsite storage. Offsite backups ensure that data is protected from local disasters, such as fires or floods, which could affect both the primary database and the backup. Using multiple backup locations, such as remote data centers or cloud storage, ensures that data remains available and recoverable even if the primary location is compromised. Backup systems should be designed to automate replication to offsite locations, ensuring that databases are backed up in real time or near real time, depending on the organization's recovery point objective (RPO) and recovery time objective (RTO).

When managing database backups, it is also important to account for database size and growth. As databases expand, the time required for backup operations can increase significantly, making it essential to continuously monitor backup performance and storage utilization. To address this, some organizations implement strategies such as database partitioning or sharding, where large databases are split into smaller, more manageable chunks. This approach allows for faster backup and recovery times by enabling parallel backups of smaller subsets of data. Additionally, organizations may consider using storage-efficient techniques such as data deduplication and compression to reduce the amount of storage required for backups and decrease the backup window.

Retention and archival of database backups are also crucial components of managing backups in cloud environments. Many organizations must retain backups for extended periods due to legal, regulatory, or business continuity requirements. Cloud storage solutions typically offer different tiers of storage, such as hot, cold, or archive storage, which can be used to optimize costs based on the frequency of access required. For example, databases that require frequent access may be backed up to hot storage, while older backups that are unlikely to be accessed regularly may be moved to more cost-effective cold or archive storage. By implementing a well-defined backup retention policy, organizations can ensure that they comply with regulatory requirements while managing storage costs effectively.

Testing database backups is another critical aspect of database management. Backups must be regularly tested to verify their integrity and ensure they can be restored when needed. This is particularly important for databases, as failures in the backup process can lead to significant data loss or application downtime. Restore tests should be performed regularly, and databases should be restored to test environments to ensure that they are functional and consistent with the original data. These tests help identify potential issues with the backup process, such as missing files, corrupt data, or incomplete backups, allowing organizations to address any problems before they impact operations.

Effective management of databases within filesystem backups requires a combination of strategy, tools, and best practices. Ensuring that database backups are consistent, secure, and reliable is essential to maintaining data integrity and supporting business continuity. By leveraging application-aware backups, using transaction logs, optimizing storage solutions, and testing backups regularly, organizations can protect their critical data and ensure that it remains available and recoverable in the event of a failure or disaster. As databases continue to grow in size and complexity, adapting backup strategies to meet these demands will remain an essential part of any organization's data protection plan.

Managing Filesystem Backups on Linux

Managing filesystem backups on Linux is an essential aspect of system administration. Linux, known for its stability and performance, is widely used in both personal and enterprise environments. Ensuring the availability of backup solutions and the integrity of data on Linux systems requires an understanding of the underlying filesystem structure, backup tools, and strategies to maintain data security and consistency. A well-structured backup strategy can protect against data loss due to hardware failures, accidental deletions, or catastrophic system errors, while also allowing for efficient recovery in a timely manner.

Linux filesystems are diverse and offer different types of support and functionality, from the widely used ext4, which is often the default, to more advanced filesystems like Btrfs, XFS, and ZFS. Understanding the specific requirements and characteristics of the filesystem in use is the first step in effectively managing backups. Each of these filesystems has its own set of features that can impact the backup strategy. For example, Btrfs offers built-in snapshot capabilities, while ext4, as a more traditional filesystem, requires external tools for creating consistent snapshots or backups. The tools and methods chosen for backups must be compatible with the filesystem to ensure data consistency and efficient management of backup data.

In Linux, the most common methods for performing backups are file-based backups, block-level backups, and image-based backups. File-based backups copy individual files or directories, which can be done using command-line utilities like tar, rsync, or cp. These methods are highly flexible and allow administrators to backup specific parts of the system rather than the entire filesystem. This approach is useful for managing the backup of specific files or directories that may change frequently. Tools like rsync are often favored in Linux environments for their efficiency, as they only transfer changed data, minimizing the amount of data that needs to be copied during incremental backups.

Block-level backups involve backing up data at the block level, which means copying data from disk blocks rather than individual files. This type of backup is typically used for creating full system backups, including the operating system, configuration files, and all other data stored on the disk. Block-level backups can be achieved using tools like dd or by utilizing LVM snapshots, which are commonly used on systems that leverage Logical Volume Manager (LVM) for managing storage. These backups are often larger and require more storage space but can be helpful for full system restores, as they preserve the state of the entire disk.

Image-based backups take a snapshot of the entire filesystem or disk and store it as a single file, which can be used to restore the system to its exact state at the time of the backup. These backups are particularly useful for disaster recovery, as they provide a complete backup of the system, including the operating system, applications, and user data. Tools like Clonezilla or partimage can be used to create disk images of a Linux system. Image-based backups allow for fast and complete restores, especially in scenarios where the system is rendered unusable due to a failure. These backups can be more time-consuming and resource-intensive, particularly when backing up large disks, but they offer the advantage of complete system recovery.

One of the primary considerations when managing filesystem backups on Linux is ensuring data consistency. Unlike traditional filesystems, which may allow data to be written while the backup process is underway, Linux systems often require more careful handling to ensure that files are not in the middle of being modified during the backup process. This can lead to inconsistent backups, where some files may be captured in their updated state while others may be partially written. To avoid this issue, Linux administrators often rely on tools like fsfreeze (for ext4 filesystems) or filesystem snapshots, particularly with advanced filesystems like Btrfs and LVM. These tools temporarily freeze the filesystem, ensuring that all data is in a consistent state before backup operations begin.

For LVM users, snapshots provide a valuable mechanism for creating consistent backups of live systems. LVM snapshots allow administrators to create a read-only or read-write copy of a logical volume at a specific point in time, which can be backed up without affecting the live system. This allows for backups of active systems without the need for downtime. However, administrators should be cautious when using LVM snapshots, as they can consume significant storage space, and the performance of the system may degrade if snapshots are held for extended periods.

In terms of remote backups, Linux systems often leverage networked storage solutions, such as NFS or SMB shares, or cloud-based backup services. Network-based backups provide the advantage of storing backup data offsite, protecting it from local disasters, hardware failures, or accidental deletion. The rsync tool, for example, is commonly used for synchronizing files between local and remote servers, making it an ideal choice for remote backups. With rsync, only the changes to files are transferred, which saves on bandwidth and reduces backup time. Additionally, cloud-based backup services are increasingly popular among Linux administrators for their scalability and cost-effectiveness. These services allow for the automatic backup of Linux systems to the cloud, where data is stored securely and can be easily restored in the event of a disaster.

While cloud backups offer numerous benefits, Linux administrators should also be aware of the potential limitations and risks, such as bandwidth constraints, latency issues, and security concerns. Encrypting backup data before transmission is essential when using cloud backup services, as it ensures that sensitive information remains secure. Linux provides various encryption tools, such as gpg or openssl, that can be used to encrypt backup data before it is transmitted to the cloud. It is also important to configure proper access controls and ensure that the cloud provider complies with relevant regulations for data protection, such as GDPR or HIPAA.

Backup retention is another critical aspect of managing filesystem backups on Linux. Over time, backup files can accumulate and consume significant amounts of storage space. Setting up automated retention policies is important to manage this growth and ensure that outdated backups are safely archived or deleted according to organizational requirements. Tools like cron can be used to automate the scheduling of backup tasks, including cleaning up older backups. Retention policies should also take into account compliance and regulatory requirements, such as those governing data retention periods in industries like healthcare or finance.

Regular backup testing is a key practice for ensuring that backup processes are functioning as expected and that data can be reliably restored when needed. Linux administrators should periodically test their backup solutions by performing full system restores or recovering specific files to verify the integrity of backup data. This helps identify potential issues with the backup system and ensures that the backup process is performing efficiently. Testing also ensures that administrators are familiar with the restoration process, which is crucial in the event of a disaster recovery scenario.

Overall, managing filesystem backups on Linux requires careful planning, a strong understanding of Linux filesystems, and the use of appropriate backup tools to ensure data consistency, security, and availability. Whether using file-based, block-level, or image-based backups, Linux administrators must select the right backup strategy based on the specific needs of their systems and applications. Regular testing, retention management, and remote storage options further enhance the effectiveness of Linux backup strategies, ensuring that organizations can recover their data swiftly and reliably in the face of failure. As technology continues to evolve, so too will the methods and tools available for Linux administrators to manage filesystem backups and ensure data protection.

Managing Filesystem Backups on Windows

Managing filesystem backups on Windows is a crucial task for system administrators, ensuring that critical data is protected and recoverable in the event of hardware failures, accidental deletions, or system crashes. Windows operating systems provide various tools and mechanisms for creating backups, and understanding how to efficiently use these tools to safeguard data is vital for businesses and individuals alike. Backup strategies on Windows need to be designed with careful attention to the specific needs of the environment, including the types of data being stored, the frequency of backups, and the overall recovery objectives.

Windows offers several built-in tools for managing backups, each with different functionalities. One of the most commonly used tools is Windows Backup and Restore, which has been a part of the operating system for many years. This tool provides both full and incremental backups of the entire system or specific files and folders. It allows users to create system image backups, which capture the entire state of the system, including the operating system, installed applications, and user data. This type of backup is useful for disaster recovery, as it allows for a complete restoration of the system to the exact state it was in at the time of the backup. The system image backup, however, can be large, and restoring from it may require significant time and storage resources.

Another powerful tool available in Windows for backup management is the File History feature, which is designed for more granular file-level backups. File History automatically backs up user files, such as documents, photos, and music, to an external drive or network location at regular intervals. This tool is particularly beneficial for protecting user-generated data, as it allows users to easily recover previous versions of files that have been accidentally modified or deleted. File History creates incremental backups, meaning that only the changes made to files since the last backup are stored, reducing storage requirements. File History is also integrated with the Windows File Explorer, allowing users to restore previous versions of files directly from the interface, providing a convenient and efficient way to manage file-level backups.

In addition to these built-in tools, Windows also supports third-party backup solutions, which often offer more advanced features and greater flexibility than the native options. Many organizations and individuals turn to third-party backup software to meet their specific needs, particularly in larger environments where backup management can become more complex. Third-party solutions typically offer features such as centralized backup management, better scheduling options, enhanced compression and encryption, and more robust disaster recovery capabilities. These tools can also provide more granular control over backup destinations, whether on local storage, networked devices, or cloud storage platforms.

When managing filesystem backups on Windows, it is important to consider the type of backup method being used. Full backups capture all selected data, including system files, applications, and user files, and create a complete copy of the data. These backups can take longer to perform, especially if the system contains large amounts of data, but they provide a comprehensive snapshot that is useful for full restores. Incremental backups, on the other hand, only back up the changes made since the last backup, whether it was full or incremental. Incremental backups are faster and more efficient in terms of storage, as they only capture the new or modified data. However, restoring from incremental backups can be more time-consuming, as all previous backups in the chain must be applied to achieve a complete restore.

Differential backups, similar to incremental backups, only capture the data that has changed since the last full backup, but unlike incremental backups, they do not require the entire chain of backups for restoration. This means that differential backups provide faster restore times compared to incremental backups but may require more storage, as they can grow larger over time. Organizations must decide on the right combination of full, incremental, and differential backups based on their recovery time objectives (RTO) and recovery point objectives (RPO), balancing backup efficiency with restore speed.

One of the primary challenges in managing filesystem backups on Windows is ensuring data consistency, particularly when backing up live systems. When a backup is being performed, the data may still be in use by running applications, making it difficult to capture a consistent snapshot of the system. Windows offers Volume Shadow Copy Service (VSS), which is a feature that allows for the creation of consistent backups of live systems by creating snapshots of the filesystem. VSS ensures that backup operations do not interfere with active data and applications, making it possible to back up open files and databases without causing corruption or inconsistencies. VSS is particularly useful when backing up databases, virtual machines, or other services that require consistency during backup operations.

Another important consideration when managing backups on Windows is the destination storage location. Windows allows backups to be stored locally on external drives or networked devices, or remotely in cloud storage. The choice of storage location depends on factors such as the size of the backup, recovery requirements, and budget. Local storage offers fast access and recovery speeds but may be vulnerable to local disasters, such as fires or theft. Remote and cloud-based storage solutions, on the other hand, offer greater resilience and redundancy, as data is stored offsite and can be accessed from anywhere. However, cloud backups may incur additional costs and can be limited by bandwidth, which may impact the time required to perform backups or restore data.

For organizations with multiple systems, it is essential to implement a centralized backup management system to ensure consistency and efficiency across all machines. Windows Server provides centralized backup tools through Windows Server Backup, which allows administrators to schedule, monitor, and manage backups for multiple servers in a networked environment. For larger enterprise environments, third-party backup solutions often provide even more comprehensive management features, including centralized control over backup policies, reporting, and integration with disaster recovery plans.

Backup retention is another critical component of backup management. Over time, backup files can accumulate, consuming valuable storage space. Without proper retention policies, organizations may end up storing unnecessary backups, leading to inefficiencies and increased costs. Retention policies define how long backup data is kept and when it is deleted or archived. For example, full backups may be retained for a longer period, while incremental backups may only be kept for a few weeks or months. Automated tools can be used to enforce retention policies, ensuring that old backups are properly managed without requiring manual intervention.

Monitoring backup operations is essential for identifying potential issues before they become critical. Windows provides event logging, which can be used to track backup success or failure. Backup software can also generate reports and notifications, alerting administrators to issues such as failed backups, insufficient storage, or missed backup schedules. Regular monitoring helps ensure that backups are completing successfully and that any problems are addressed promptly to avoid data loss.

Effective filesystem backup management on Windows requires understanding the available tools and technologies, such as Windows Backup and Restore, File History, and third-party solutions. By combining full, incremental, and differential backups, leveraging Volume Shadow Copy Service for consistency, and carefully considering storage locations, organizations can create a comprehensive backup strategy. Regular monitoring and implementing proper retention policies help ensure that backup operations remain efficient and secure, providing a reliable safety net for data protection and disaster recovery. Whether for personal use or enterprise environments, managing filesystem backups on Windows is essential to safeguarding critical data and ensuring business continuity.

Backup Software: Open Source vs Commercial Solutions

Backup software is a critical component of any data protection strategy, ensuring that important data is regularly backed up and easily recoverable in the event of hardware failure, accidental deletion, or other catastrophic events. As the need for data protection grows, businesses and individuals must evaluate the best solutions for their backup needs. One of the key decisions in this process is choosing between open-source backup software and commercial solutions. Both options offer advantages and drawbacks, and the choice largely depends on the specific needs of the organization, available resources, and the level of support required.

Open-source backup software is typically free to use and offers users the flexibility to modify and customize the software to suit their needs. Many open-source backup tools have been developed by a community of users and developers, which means they are often highly flexible and capable of handling a wide range of backup tasks. Tools like Bacula,

Duplicity, and rsync are examples of open-source backup solutions that are widely used for both personal and enterprise-level backups. Open-source solutions often provide a strong foundation for users who have specific technical requirements and are looking to integrate backup software into existing systems or workflows.

One of the main advantages of open-source backup software is its cost. Since it is usually free to use, it offers an affordable option for individuals, small businesses, or organizations with limited budgets. For many small to medium-sized enterprises (SMEs), open-source solutions offer a way to implement a robust backup strategy without the financial commitment required by commercial software. Additionally, open-source software provides the opportunity to customize the solution to fit unique needs, allowing organizations to modify the code or functionality to suit specific backup scenarios, such as integrating with proprietary systems or adding specialized features.

Despite its advantages, open-source backup software comes with its own set of challenges. One of the primary drawbacks is the lack of formal support. While community forums and user groups often provide assistance, users of open-source backup solutions may not have access to professional, dedicated support channels. This can be problematic for businesses that require timely and reliable support, particularly in mission-critical environments where downtime is not an option. When issues arise with open-source backup software, organizations may need to rely on internal IT staff or third-party contractors to resolve them, which can incur additional costs and delays.

Another challenge with open-source solutions is that they often require a higher level of technical expertise to implement and manage. While many open-source backup tools offer powerful features, they are typically less user-friendly than commercial alternatives. Open-source solutions often come with limited graphical user interfaces (GUIs) or require command-line interaction, which may be a barrier for users who are not familiar with Linux or system administration. Additionally, while open-source tools may be highly customizable, this customization can require time and technical resources to develop and maintain, which can be a significant burden for smaller organizations without dedicated IT teams.

On the other hand, commercial backup software typically comes with a range of built-in features designed to streamline the backup process and make it easier to manage. These solutions often offer user-friendly interfaces, automated backups, and pre-configured templates that reduce the time and effort required to implement a backup strategy. Commercial solutions such as Veeam, Acronis, and Veritas provide extensive documentation, support, and training, ensuring that users can quickly get up and running with minimal configuration. For organizations with limited technical expertise or those who need to deploy backups quickly, commercial software can be a more attractive option.

Commercial backup software also provides reliable customer support, including dedicated technical assistance, software updates, and patches. This is particularly valuable for businesses that rely on their backup systems for business continuity and cannot afford downtime. The ability to contact a support team when issues arise ensures that problems are resolved quickly and efficiently, minimizing disruptions. Furthermore, commercial backup solutions often include additional features such as disaster recovery, encryption, and cloud integration, which can provide enhanced data protection and recovery options.

However, the main disadvantage of commercial backup software is the cost. Licensing fees for commercial backup software can be expensive, especially for larger organizations or those with large amounts of data to back up. Pricing structures can vary widely depending on the software, with some vendors charging based on the number of devices or users, while others charge based on the amount of data stored. For small businesses or individuals, the costs associated with commercial solutions may be prohibitive, making open-source alternatives a more viable option. However, for larger enterprises or businesses with complex backup needs, the additional features, support, and reliability offered by commercial backup solutions may justify the higher cost.

Another consideration when choosing between open-source and commercial backup solutions is the scalability of the software. Commercial solutions tend to be more scalable, offering features that allow businesses to easily expand their backup infrastructure as their data grows. For example, many commercial solutions offer cloud integration, allowing businesses to scale their storage capacity without having to invest in additional on-premises hardware. Open-source solutions, while customizable, may require significant effort and resources to scale effectively, particularly when dealing with large volumes of data or complex environments.

The speed of deployment is another factor that often favors commercial backup software. Commercial solutions are typically designed to be installed and configured with minimal effort, and vendors often provide pre-configured systems or cloud-based options that can be up and running in a short amount of time. This is beneficial for businesses that need to implement backup systems quickly and without significant delays. In contrast, open-source backup software may require more time to deploy, as users need to configure and customize the software to meet their specific needs, particularly in more complex or large-scale environments.

For businesses that prioritize a balance between cost-effectiveness and feature richness, hybrid approaches are increasingly common. Many organizations combine open-source backup solutions with commercial solutions to leverage the benefits of both. For example, open-source software may be used for routine backups, while commercial software is deployed for more critical data or disaster recovery purposes. This hybrid approach allows businesses to optimize costs while ensuring that their most critical data is protected with the reliability and support offered by commercial solutions.

When deciding between open-source and commercial backup software, organizations must evaluate their specific needs, available resources, and the level of support required. For smaller organizations or individuals with limited budgets and technical expertise, open-source solutions offer an affordable and flexible option. However, businesses with more complex backup needs, a large volume of data, or critical uptime requirements may find that commercial solutions offer better support, more features, and a higher level of reliability. The right choice ultimately depends on the organization's priorities, whether that be minimizing costs, maximizing scalability, or ensuring comprehensive support for disaster recovery.

Using Backup Software for Automation

Backup automation has become an essential component of modern IT infrastructure, allowing organizations to ensure that their data is consistently protected without the need for manual intervention. Traditional backup methods often required administrators to initiate backups manually, a time-consuming and error-prone process. However, with the advancement of backup software and automation tools, businesses can now schedule and manage backups automatically, ensuring data integrity, reducing human error, and increasing operational efficiency. Automation not only simplifies backup processes but also ensures that critical data is regularly backed up, minimizing the risk of data loss due to unforeseen circumstances such as hardware failures, ransomware attacks, or accidental deletions.

The key advantage of using backup software for automation is its ability to schedule backup tasks according to predefined intervals. Instead of relying on administrators to remember to initiate backups, the software can be configured to automatically perform backups at specific times, whether daily, weekly, or monthly. For example, an organization may choose to perform a full backup of critical systems every Sunday evening, followed by incremental backups every weekday night. This level of scheduling flexibility ensures that backups occur regularly, without the need for constant monitoring or intervention by IT staff. Scheduling backups also ensures that they are performed during off-peak hours, reducing the impact on system performance and ensuring that users are not interrupted during their workday.

In addition to scheduling, automation also enables backup software to perform a wide range of tasks without manual input. These tasks can include verifying the success of the backup process, checking for data integrity, managing storage space, and even sending alerts to administrators if a backup fails or encounters issues. By automating these processes, backup software reduces the administrative burden on IT teams, allowing them to focus on more strategic initiatives while ensuring that backups are consistently completed. Automated verification and reporting help ensure that backups are complete and free of errors, minimizing the risk of restoring corrupted or incomplete data.

One of the key features of backup software for automation is its ability to perform incremental and differential backups. These types of backups are highly efficient, as they only back up the data that has changed since the last backup, reducing the amount of data that needs to be transferred and stored. Incremental backups only include data that has changed since the previous backup, whether full or incremental, while differential backups include all data that has changed since the last full backup. Automating these processes ensures that backups are completed quickly and efficiently, without consuming excessive storage space or bandwidth. Backup software can be configured to automatically select the appropriate backup type based on the organization's needs, ensuring that backups are performed in the most efficient manner possible.

Cloud-based backup solutions have further enhanced the benefits of backup automation. With cloud storage, organizations no longer need to rely solely on physical backup devices or on-premises infrastructure. Cloud backup software can automatically send data to remote servers, providing offsite protection against local disasters such as fires, floods, or theft. The integration of cloud-based backup software with automation tools allows organizations to easily manage backups in hybrid or multi-cloud environments, with automated workflows that move backup data between local storage and cloud destinations. For instance, critical data can be backed up locally for faster access, while less frequently accessed data can be moved to a cloud storage solution to reduce costs.

Backup automation also plays a critical role in disaster recovery strategies. In the event of a system failure or data loss, automated backups ensure that the most recent data is available for restoration. Automated backup software can be integrated with disaster recovery plans to ensure that backup copies are easily accessible, and recovery procedures are streamlined. Many backup solutions offer automated recovery options, allowing administrators to quickly restore entire systems or individual files with minimal downtime. For instance, organizations can automate the creation of recovery points at regular intervals, ensuring that they have access to a reliable backup copy for quick and efficient restoration when needed. By automating the backup and recovery process, businesses can reduce recovery time objectives (RTOs) and recovery point objectives (RPOs), ensuring that critical systems are restored swiftly and with minimal data loss.

Data security is another area where backup automation plays a vital role. As businesses handle increasing amounts of sensitive and personal data, ensuring that backups are secure is paramount. Automated backup software often includes built-in encryption options, ensuring that backup data is securely encrypted both at rest and during transfer. This protects sensitive information from unauthorized access and ensures compliance with data privacy regulations such as the General Data Protection Regulation (GDPR) and the Health Insurance Portability and Accountability Act (HIPAA). Automated encryption also reduces the risk of human error, as administrators do not need to manually apply encryption to each backup set. By automating encryption, organizations can ensure that all backup data is protected from potential threats, whether it is stored on local devices or in the cloud.

Another benefit of using backup software for automation is its ability to scale with an organization's growth. As data volumes increase over time, automated backup solutions can be adjusted to accommodate larger datasets. Backup software can be configured to automatically manage storage resources, moving older backups to lower-cost storage tiers, archiving infrequently accessed data, or deleting backups that are no longer needed. This scalability ensures that backup processes remain efficient, even as the organization's data grows. For example, backup software can be set to automatically migrate older backups to tape or cloud storage, ensuring that storage resources are used effectively while keeping recent backups readily available.

Furthermore, automated backup systems can be integrated with other IT management tools to provide comprehensive monitoring and alerting capabilities. Backup software can be configured to send automated notifications and alerts when backups fail, when storage is nearing capacity, or when other issues arise. These alerts can be sent via email, text message, or integration with a centralized monitoring system, ensuring that administrators are promptly informed of any backup-related problems. Automated alerts enable IT teams to take immediate action to resolve issues before they lead to data loss or system downtime. This proactive approach to backup management enhances the overall reliability and effectiveness of the backup system.

The use of backup software for automation ultimately reduces the complexity of data protection processes. By automating the scheduling, execution, and verification of backups, organizations can ensure that their data is consistently protected with minimal manual effort. This leads to a more reliable backup process, minimizes the risk of human error, and ensures that backup tasks are executed on time, every time. Automated backup systems also improve operational efficiency by allowing IT teams to focus on other critical tasks while ensuring that data remains safe and recoverable. Whether for individual users, small businesses, or large enterprises, backup automation provides a streamlined, efficient solution to data protection that meets the demands of modern IT environments.

Optimizing Backup Speed and Efficiency

In today's fast-paced digital world, data is one of the most valuable assets for organizations and individuals alike. As the volume of data continues to increase, ensuring that data is backed up quickly and efficiently becomes paramount. Efficient backups not only save time and resources but also ensure that data protection does not interfere with the performance of primary systems. Optimizing backup speed and efficiency is crucial for maintaining business continuity, reducing downtime, and minimizing the impact of data loss events. However, achieving this balance requires a combination of strategies, tools, and technologies that work together to streamline the backup process while ensuring data integrity and availability.

One of the most fundamental aspects of optimizing backup speed and efficiency is understanding the types of backups being performed. There are several methods for backing up data, including full backups, incremental backups, and differential backups, each with its own implications for speed and resource usage. Full backups copy all data to the backup medium, and while they are comprehensive, they can be time-consuming and storage-intensive, particularly for large datasets. Incremental backups, on the other hand, only back up the changes made since the last backup, reducing the amount of data transferred and stored. Differential backups capture changes since the last full backup, providing a middle ground between the efficiency of incremental backups and the completeness of full backups. By choosing the appropriate backup type based on the frequency of changes and the required recovery time, organizations can significantly improve backup efficiency.

Another critical factor in backup speed is the technology used for transferring and storing data. Network bandwidth plays a key role in the speed of backups, especially in environments where data is being transferred across networks. For instance, backing up large datasets to remote servers or cloud storage can be hindered by slow internet connections. To overcome this, it is essential to optimize network usage by scheduling backups during off-peak hours, ensuring that backup tasks do not compete with other essential network traffic. In addition, using compression and deduplication technologies can reduce the amount of data that needs to be transferred. Compression reduces the size of the backup files, while deduplication eliminates redundant data, ensuring that only unique information is stored. Both of these techniques can help minimize bandwidth usage, improving backup speed and efficiency.

Deduplication, in particular, plays a significant role in optimizing backup efficiency. Many organizations store large amounts of similar or identical data across various systems, which leads to redundant backups. Deduplication identifies and eliminates these redundant files or data blocks, ensuring that only unique data is backed up. This can greatly reduce the amount of storage required, as well as the time needed to back up data. Deduplication can be applied at the source or target level. Source-side deduplication occurs before data is transferred to the backup medium, while target-side deduplication occurs after the data has been received. Both methods help improve backup efficiency, especially in environments with large amounts of duplicate data.

In addition to data compression and deduplication, the storage medium itself plays a crucial role in backup performance. Traditional hard drives (HDDs) have been largely replaced by solid-state drives (SSDs) in many environments due to the latter's faster read and write speeds. Using SSDs for backup storage can significantly speed up both backup and restore processes, reducing the overall time required to complete backups. For organizations with large-scale data backup requirements, implementing storage solutions with faster write speeds can have a profound impact on backup efficiency. Furthermore, hybrid storage solutions, which combine both SSDs and HDDs, offer an ideal balance between performance and cost. Frequently accessed or critical data can be stored on SSDs for faster backups, while less critical data can be placed on HDDs to reduce storage costs.

Cloud-based backups are increasingly popular due to their scalability and offsite data protection capabilities. However, backing up data to the cloud introduces new challenges related to speed. Cloud storage providers typically offer various tiers of storage, from high-performance solutions for frequently accessed data to cold storage for archival purposes. Choosing the appropriate storage tier based on the frequency of access and backup requirements can help optimize both backup speed and cost. Additionally, cloud providers often offer features such as bandwidth throttling and multi-threaded transfers, which can help manage the speed of data uploads and ensure that backups do not overwhelm the network. Utilizing these features effectively can make cloud backups faster and more efficient, particularly when dealing with large datasets.

Another strategy for optimizing backup efficiency is the use of snapshot technology. A snapshot is a point-in-time copy of the data that allows backups to be taken without affecting the live system. Snapshots provide an efficient way to back up large volumes of data quickly, as they do not require copying all the data immediately. Instead, they capture a reference to the data, which can then be backed up incrementally. Many modern file systems, such as ZFS, Btrfs, and LVM, support snapshot technology, enabling organizations to create backups of running systems without significant performance degradation. Snapshots also facilitate faster restores, as they capture the entire state of the system at a specific point in time, reducing the need to manually locate and restore individual files.

The frequency of backups also plays a role in optimizing efficiency. Performing backups too frequently can lead to unnecessary use of resources, while performing them too infrequently can result in larger backup sizes and slower restore times. To strike the right balance, organizations can implement backup policies that are tailored to their data needs. For example, critical data may be backed up more frequently, while less important data can be backed up less often. Additionally, implementing policies that include regular full backups followed by incremental backups can help reduce the amount of time required for each backup while ensuring that the data is always protected.

Automation of the backup process can further enhance speed and efficiency. Manual backups can be prone to human error and may be forgotten, leading to gaps in data protection. By automating backup schedules, organizations can ensure that backups occur consistently and without delay. Many modern backup solutions provide robust automation features, allowing administrators to set schedules, configure retention policies, and even receive alerts if a backup fails. This not only saves time but also ensures that backups are performed regularly without requiring constant supervision. Automation also enables backup processes to occur during off-peak hours, reducing the impact on system performance.

One additional technique for optimizing backup speed and efficiency is data prioritization. In many environments, not all data is equally critical or time-sensitive. By classifying data based on its importance and frequency of access, organizations can prioritize the backup of critical data and delay the backup of less important data. This approach allows for more efficient use of storage and bandwidth resources, as high-priority data can be backed up first, while less important data can be scheduled for later. This prioritization strategy can be particularly useful in large environments with diverse data types and backup requirements.

In conclusion, optimizing backup speed and efficiency requires a multifaceted approach that combines the right tools, technologies, and strategies. By leveraging methods such as incremental and differential backups, compression, deduplication, and snapshot technology, organizations can significantly improve the speed of their backups while reducing storage requirements. Choosing the right storage medium, utilizing cloud backup features, and automating backup processes further contribute to more efficient data protection. With the increasing amount of data organizations need to manage, optimizing backup performance is not just a matter of convenience, but an essential part of ensuring that data is consistently protected and recoverable in the event of a disaster.

Filesystem Integrity Checks and Verification

Ensuring the integrity of a filesystem is critical to maintaining data reliability, availability, and security. Filesystem integrity refers to the consistency and correctness of the data stored on a disk, ensuring that it has not been corrupted, lost, or altered in an unintended manner. Filesystem integrity checks and verification play a vital role in safeguarding data against corruption, ensuring that files and directories are stored and accessed properly, and confirming that the system is functioning as expected. Regularly verifying the integrity of filesystems is a key practice for preventing data loss, avoiding downtime, and ensuring that recovery procedures are effective when needed.

Filesystems are responsible for managing how data is stored and retrieved on storage devices. Over time, filesystems can become vulnerable to corruption due to various factors, including hardware failures, software bugs, power outages, or human error. Data corruption can occur at multiple levels, ranging from a single file being altered or deleted, to a complete filesystem becoming unusable. In many cases, the corruption may go unnoticed until a restore is required, highlighting the importance of regular checks to detect and correct issues before they escalate.

Filesystem integrity checks are typically performed by specialized utilities designed to examine the structure and metadata of the filesystem. These utilities can detect and repair issues such as corrupted files, missing or incorrect metadata, or mismatched file pointers. One of the most widely used tools for this purpose in Linux environments is fsck, short for filesystem check. The fsck tool examines the filesystem's metadata to ensure that all files and directories are correctly linked and that there are no inconsistencies. It also checks the integrity of file allocation tables and inodes, which are crucial to the proper functioning of a filesystem. In Windows, the chkdsk tool performs similar tasks by scanning and fixing errors within the file system and the metadata structures that store information about files.

Filesystem checks can be initiated manually or scheduled to run automatically at regular intervals. For instance, Linux administrators may set up periodic checks using cron jobs or systemd timers to ensure that their filesystems are regularly scanned for integrity issues. Similarly, in Windows, the chkdsk tool can be scheduled to run at startup or be manually initiated. These checks typically run in the background to minimize disruption to system operations, but in some cases, they may require the system to be unmounted or in a read-only state, particularly if the integrity issues are severe.

While filesystem integrity checks are vital for detecting and correcting issues, verification involves confirming that the system and data are functioning as expected after the check has been performed. Verification processes ensure that any repairs made during the integrity check are successful and that no new issues have been introduced. One common method for verifying filesystem integrity is through checksums or hash functions. A checksum is a small-sized piece of data derived from a larger data set, which acts as a unique identifier for the data. When performing an integrity check, the system compares the current checksum of a file or block of data with a previously stored checksum. If the two checksums match, the data is considered intact; if they differ, the data has been altered or corrupted.

Many modern filesystems, such as ZFS and Btrfs, have built-in features that enhance both integrity checking and verification. ZFS, for instance, employs end-to-end checksumming, meaning that every block of data and metadata is checksummed as it is written to disk. ZFS then continuously verifies the checksums during reads and can automatically detect and correct any corruption by using its redundant copies of data. Similarly, Btrfs provides built-in checksumming for data and metadata, and it allows for self-healing by leveraging the system's RAID-like redundancy features. These advanced filesystems provide an extra layer of protection by ensuring data integrity is maintained at all times, with automatic error correction features that reduce the need for manual intervention.

Filesystem verification also involves monitoring the overall health of the filesystem. Filesystem health checks can detect not only data corruption but also issues related to disk performance, bad sectors, or other hardware failures that may affect data integrity. Many tools, such as smartctl in Linux or the built-in Windows Disk Management tool, can monitor the health of storage devices by analyzing the SMART (Self-Monitoring, Analysis, and Reporting Technology) data. These tools provide insight into the condition of the physical hardware and can alert administrators to issues like increasing numbers of bad sectors or deteriorating performance, which may impact the integrity of stored data.

Another crucial aspect of verifying filesystem integrity is ensuring that backups are also consistently verified. Backups play a central role in data protection strategies, but they can be rendered ineffective if the integrity of the backup data is compromised. During the backup process, it is important to check the integrity of the backup itself to ensure that it is an accurate and reliable copy of the original data. Many modern backup solutions offer built-in integrity verification features that compare the source data with the backup copy, ensuring that the backup has been successfully created without errors or corruption. Regular verification of backups, combined with filesystem integrity checks, helps ensure that both the original data and its backups remain reliable and consistent.

In complex systems with multiple filesystems or distributed storage environments, verifying filesystem integrity becomes more challenging. In these cases, administrators must implement specialized monitoring tools to track the health and consistency of each filesystem. Distributed systems may require centralized monitoring platforms that aggregate and display data from multiple sources, allowing administrators to quickly identify and address integrity issues across different machines or environments. Additionally, organizations with large-scale storage systems, such as network-attached storage (NAS) or storage area networks (SAN), may need to implement automated integrity verification processes that scan and verify large volumes of data in a timely and efficient manner.

Filesystem integrity checks and verification are critical for ensuring the long-term stability and reliability of data storage systems. While tools like fsck and chkdsk provide essential utilities for checking and repairing filesystem issues, advanced filesystems such as ZFS and Btrfs offer additional features like built-in checksumming and self-healing capabilities, which further enhance data protection. Regular integrity checks and verification are necessary practices for maintaining data consistency and minimizing the risk of data loss or corruption. As data volumes increase and systems become more complex, organizations must adopt robust strategies for verifying and maintaining filesystem integrity to protect valuable data assets. With the right tools, processes, and monitoring in place, administrators can ensure that their systems remain stable, reliable, and ready for recovery in the event of a failure.

Impact of Filesystem Design on Backup Strategy

The design of a filesystem plays a fundamental role in shaping an effective backup strategy. Filesystems are responsible for organizing and managing data on storage devices, and they significantly impact how data is stored, accessed, and backed up. Whether in a personal computing environment or a large-scale enterprise infrastructure, understanding the intricacies of filesystem design is crucial for ensuring that backups are efficient, reliable, and capable of meeting recovery objectives. Filesystem design influences backup frequency, the type of backups used, recovery times, storage requirements, and overall system performance during backup operations.

One of the primary factors that filesystem design affects is the granularity of backups. A filesystem organizes data into files and directories, and depending on its structure, backing up individual files or entire volumes may have different implications. For example, a filesystem that stores files in large blocks may result in significant storage overhead when performing incremental backups, as even minor changes to a file could result in large blocks being backed up. On the other hand, filesystems that employ more advanced storage techniques, such as journaling or copy-on-write mechanisms, may enable more efficient backups by reducing the size of the data that needs to be transferred or stored during an incremental backup. A filesystem's organization can therefore determine whether it is more beneficial to use full backups, incremental backups, or differential backups to maintain a balance between data protection and storage efficiency.

The type of filesystem used also influences how backup solutions interact with the system during the backup process. For example, in filesystems like NTFS, which is commonly used in Windows environments, backups often require the use of system-level utilities that interact with the filesystem's metadata to ensure data consistency. In contrast, more advanced filesystems like Btrfs or ZFS offer built-in snapshot capabilities, which allow administrators to create point-in-time copies of the filesystem without interrupting normal system operations. These snapshots can then be backed up without the risk of data corruption or inconsistency. The use of snapshots can significantly reduce backup time, as it allows for fast, consistent backups without requiring the system to be offline or paused.

Another critical aspect of filesystem design that impacts backup strategy is the level of redundancy built into the filesystem. Filesystems like ZFS and Btrfs are designed to support data redundancy at the filesystem level, offering features such as data mirroring and parity-based storage. These features ensure that data is protected from hardware failure, but they also influence how backups should be managed. In environments where data redundancy is already built into the filesystem, administrators may choose to prioritize backing up critical data rather than backing up entire volumes or disks. However, it is important to consider how the redundancy works in conjunction with backup strategies, as some of these features may reduce the need for frequent backups of certain data. For instance, in a system using ZFS with mirrored volumes, the data may already have multiple copies stored across different disks, making it possible to tailor the backup strategy to focus on other aspects of the system, such as configuration files or database snapshots, rather than duplicating data that is already protected.

Filesystem performance is another area that plays a significant role in backup strategy. The performance characteristics of the filesystem impact both the speed and efficiency of backup operations. A filesystem that is optimized for high-speed access, such as XFS or ext4, may perform better during backup operations compared to a filesystem designed for more complex data integrity features, such as ZFS. A filesystem's input/output operations per second (IOPS), read and write speeds, and latency all influence how long it takes to perform backups, particularly in large environments with significant data volumes. When designing a backup strategy, administrators need to account for these performance factors, ensuring that backups are scheduled during off-peak hours or that sufficient system resources are allocated to backup processes to avoid performance bottlenecks.

The choice of filesystem also impacts the storage efficiency of backup solutions. Filesystem features such as compression, deduplication, and data pooling can affect the amount of storage required for backups. Some filesystems, like Btrfs and ZFS, have built-in support for compression and deduplication, which can significantly reduce the amount of data that needs to be stored. Deduplication, for example, identifies and removes duplicate data blocks across the filesystem, ensuring that only unique data is backed up. This can be particularly advantageous in environments where there is a large amount of redundant data, such as virtual machine backups or environments with many similar files. Filesystem-level compression further reduces the size of the backup data, which can help organizations optimize storage costs and improve the efficiency of backup operations.

In addition to storage efficiency, the filesystem's design influences the restore process. For example, filesystems with advanced features like snapshots and replication often allow for more efficient and faster restores, as administrators can restore the system to a specific point in time rather than restoring data from incremental backups. In systems with traditional filesystems that lack such features, restoring from backup may require a more manual and time-consuming process, particularly if the backup consists of multiple incremental or differential backups. The ability to restore data quickly and accurately is a critical component of a backup strategy, and the design of the filesystem can either streamline or complicate this process. Filesystems with integrated tools for handling restoration, such as ZFS or Btrfs, are often preferred in environments where rapid recovery is essential.

The level of complexity and the administrative overhead of managing backups can also be influenced by filesystem design. For instance, traditional filesystems such as ext4 or NTFS may require additional third-party tools to perform efficient backups, manage snapshots, or verify the consistency of data. More advanced filesystems like ZFS, on the other hand, offer built-in support for many of these features, reducing the need for third-party tools and streamlining the backup and recovery process. However, these advanced filesystems also require a greater level of expertise to configure and manage, and may not be as widely supported in all environments. Therefore, administrators must consider not only the features and capabilities of the filesystem but also the technical expertise required to implement and maintain an effective backup strategy.

Filesystem design also impacts disaster recovery planning. In environments where uptime is critical, administrators may opt for filesystems that support real-time replication or distributed file systems that provide seamless failover capabilities. These features ensure that backup data is available even in the event of a system failure, making it easier to restore operations quickly. Replication technologies allow for real-time copies of data to be stored across multiple locations, ensuring that data is protected from local disasters such as fires, floods, or hardware failures. Backup strategies in such environments need to account for the seamless integration of replication and disaster recovery tools, making it possible to restore data quickly with minimal downtime.

Ultimately, the design of the filesystem plays a central role in shaping an effective backup strategy. It determines how data is organized, stored, and accessed, and influences key factors such as backup frequency, storage efficiency, performance, and restore times. By understanding the characteristics of the filesystem in use, administrators can develop tailored backup solutions that maximize efficiency, reduce downtime, and ensure data availability. Filesystem design and backup strategy must work hand in hand, with each influencing the other to ensure that data is consistently protected and recoverable when needed.

Managing Incremental Backups for Large Datasets

Managing incremental backups for large datasets is a vital part of an effective data protection strategy, particularly as data continues to grow in size and complexity. Incremental backups, unlike full backups, only capture the data that has changed since the last backup was performed. This approach is highly efficient and reduces the time and storage requirements compared to traditional full backups. However, when dealing with large datasets, there are unique challenges that require careful planning, consideration of tools, and an understanding of the trade-offs involved. By properly managing incremental backups, organizations can ensure that their data is reliably backed up without consuming excessive resources or taking up unnecessary storage space.

One of the primary benefits of incremental backups is the reduction in storage space and the amount of data transferred. For large datasets, performing full backups on a regular basis can be resource-intensive, both in terms of time and storage capacity. In contrast, incremental backups only capture the changes made since the last backup, whether that was a full or incremental backup. This ensures that only the modified or newly created data is included in the backup, significantly reducing the amount of data to be backed up. For example, if an organization has a large database with millions of records, performing a full backup would require copying the entire dataset, whereas an incremental backup would only back up the records that have changed or been added since the last backup.

However, managing incremental backups for large datasets is not without its challenges. One of the biggest hurdles is ensuring that the backup chain is maintained properly. Since incremental backups rely on the previous backup (whether full or incremental), a failure or corruption in one backup can lead to data loss. For example, if a particular incremental backup is corrupted or lost, the system may be unable to restore the data from subsequent backups, as the restore process depends on the chain of incremental backups. To mitigate this risk, it is essential to establish a robust backup strategy that includes proper monitoring, verification, and redundancy. Some organizations implement periodic full backups alongside incremental backups to break the backup chain and ensure that the system can still recover from a failure in the backup sequence.

Another challenge when managing incremental backups for large datasets is the time it takes to perform the backups. While incremental backups are faster than full backups, as they only capture changes, the sheer size of the dataset can still cause performance issues. Large datasets often involve numerous files, applications, or systems, and the process of identifying and backing up the changed data can be slow. This is particularly true in environments where the data is spread across multiple servers or storage devices. To address this, organizations can use techniques such as data deduplication, compression, and parallel processing to improve the speed of incremental backups. Deduplication ensures that only unique data is stored, while compression reduces the amount of data that needs to be transferred. Parallel processing allows for multiple backup tasks to be performed simultaneously, further speeding up the process.

Another critical aspect of managing incremental backups for large datasets is handling the frequency of backups. While it is tempting to schedule incremental backups frequently to capture every change, this can lead to an overwhelming number of backup files that are difficult to manage. A well-balanced backup schedule should be established, taking into account the frequency of data changes and the business's recovery objectives. For instance, an organization may choose to perform a full backup on a weekly basis, with incremental backups scheduled daily. This strategy ensures that the most recent data is always backed up, while still maintaining an efficient use of storage and backup resources. Additionally, the backup schedule should be aligned with the organization's recovery point objectives (RPOs) and recovery time objectives (RTOs), ensuring that the frequency of backups supports the desired recovery goals.

One of the main benefits of incremental backups is the ability to quickly restore data to the most recent point in time. Since only the changes since the last backup are stored, restoring from incremental backups is typically faster than restoring from full backups, which require restoring large volumes of data. However, the process of restoring data from incremental backups can be more complex, as each incremental backup must be applied in sequence to fully restore the data. For large datasets, this can lead to extended recovery times if the backup chain is long. To improve recovery speed, organizations should implement backup solutions that allow for quick identification and retrieval of the necessary backups. Some advanced backup tools support synthetic full backups, which combine the latest incremental backups with the previous full backup to create a new, complete backup file. This allows for faster restores, as only the most recent synthetic full backup is needed, rather than applying all incremental backups in the chain.

Data integrity is another important consideration when managing incremental backups for large datasets. As the size of the dataset grows, so does the potential for errors or corruption in the backup files. To ensure that backups are reliable, it is essential to implement regular integrity checks to verify the accuracy of the data. This can include verifying checksums or hashes to ensure that the data in the backup matches the original data. Many backup solutions offer built-in integrity verification tools that can automatically check the consistency of the backup files. Additionally, organizations should test the restore process periodically to ensure that the backup data can be recovered successfully and completely.

In large-scale environments, the management of incremental backups becomes even more complex due to the distribution of data across multiple locations, servers, or storage devices. To streamline the management of incremental backups, organizations should consider implementing a centralized backup management system. This system can automate the scheduling of backups, track the status of each backup, and provide reports on the success or failure of each backup job. Centralized backup management can also help with version control, ensuring that the correct version of the data is restored during a disaster recovery event. In addition, centralized systems can help organizations scale their backup strategy as data volumes grow, ensuring that backup tasks are performed efficiently across a large and complex infrastructure.

As large datasets continue to grow, the need for efficient incremental backup management becomes more critical. Implementing a solid backup strategy that includes incremental backups, combined with appropriate tools for performance optimization, storage management, and data verification, can help organizations maintain an efficient and reliable backup system. With the right tools and strategies in place, incremental backups can provide a cost-effective and efficient way to protect large datasets, ensuring that data is consistently available for recovery while minimizing the impact on system performance and storage requirements.

Handling Filesystem Growth and Scaling Backup Solutions

As data volumes continue to increase, the need for efficient management and backup solutions becomes more critical. Filesystem growth presents a series of challenges for system administrators, especially when it comes to ensuring that data is consistently protected, recoverable, and scalable. Scaling backup solutions to accommodate expanding filesystems requires careful planning and the integration of strategies that can evolve with the organization's growing data needs. As storage requirements increase, so too must the backup infrastructure, ensuring that it can handle larger datasets without compromising performance, efficiency, or reliability.

The first challenge in handling filesystem growth is understanding how data is structured and organized within the filesystem. As filesystems grow, the amount of data they manage increases, which can lead to performance bottlenecks. This growth can occur at various levels, from the number of files being stored to the sheer size of the data itself. Large filesystems can include a mix of various data types, such as databases, application files, and user data, each with its own set of backup requirements. When scaling backup solutions for larger filesystems, it is essential to understand the nature of the data being backed up, as well as the frequency of changes to that data. For example, some files may change frequently and need to be backed up more often, while others, such as archival data, may remain static for extended periods and only need occasional backups.

As filesystems grow, the time required to perform backups also increases, which can lead to performance issues. Traditional backup methods may become inefficient as the volume of data grows, particularly for full backups that involve copying all files in the filesystem. Incremental or differential backups can help address this issue by only backing up changes made since the last backup. However, even incremental backups can become slow as the dataset expands, and the backup process may still consume significant system resources. To scale backup solutions effectively, organizations must implement tools and strategies that can handle larger volumes of data without negatively impacting system performance. These tools often include advanced features such as parallel processing, deduplication, and compression, which help optimize backup speed and reduce storage requirements.

One of the most important considerations when scaling backup solutions is the selection of an appropriate storage infrastructure. As filesystems grow, so does the amount of storage required for backups. A small business may start with a local disk-based backup system, but as data grows, the need for a more scalable solution becomes evident. For large enterprises with vast amounts of data, using cloud storage or network-attached storage (NAS) can provide the scalability needed to accommodate growth. Cloud-based backup solutions offer virtually unlimited storage capacity, allowing organizations to scale their backup infrastructure without worrying about physical storage limitations. In addition, cloud providers often offer redundancy and geographic distribution of data, further enhancing data protection. However, while cloud storage provides scalability, it also introduces new challenges, such as bandwidth limitations, data transfer costs, and the need to manage encryption and security during transmission.

As filesystems scale, the complexity of backup management increases. Managing backups for large datasets can be cumbersome without the proper tools and processes in place. Centralized backup management solutions are essential for ensuring that backups are performed consistently across all systems and storage devices. These systems provide administrators with the ability to schedule backups, monitor their status, and manage storage resources in a single interface. Centralized backup management solutions can also integrate with other IT management tools, providing a comprehensive view of the backup infrastructure and enabling more efficient management. Automated backup scheduling, status reporting, and alerting systems can further streamline backup operations, reducing the need for manual intervention and minimizing the risk of human error.

Data deduplication is another key strategy for scaling backup solutions. As data grows, the risk of storing redundant copies of the same information increases. Deduplication technology identifies and eliminates duplicate data, ensuring that only unique data is stored in backup systems. This can significantly reduce the amount of storage required for backups and improve the efficiency of the backup process. Deduplication can be performed either at the source, before data is transmitted, or at the target, after the data has been received by the backup system. Source-side deduplication reduces network bandwidth usage, as it eliminates duplicates before they are transmitted over the network, while target-side deduplication focuses on reducing storage requirements after the data has been backed up.

Another essential aspect of scaling backup solutions for large filesystems is the ability to perform incremental backups efficiently. As filesystems grow, the number of files and directories being backed up increases, which can slow down the backup process. Incremental backups help address this by only backing up changes made since the last backup. However, with larger datasets, managing incremental backups can become complex. To handle this complexity, organizations can implement features such as backup chains or synthetic full backups. Backup chains allow incremental backups to be applied sequentially, while synthetic full backups combine the latest incremental backups with the most recent full backup to create a new, complete backup. This can reduce the number of incremental backups that need to be processed during a restore operation, speeding up recovery times.

When scaling backup solutions, it is also essential to consider the backup and recovery objectives. Recovery Time Objectives (RTO) and Recovery Point Objectives (RPO) are key metrics that help determine the frequency of backups and the time required to restore data. As filesystems grow, organizations may need to adjust their backup schedules to meet stricter RTO and RPO requirements. For example, an organization with a rapidly growing database may need to back up the database more frequently to meet its recovery objectives, while other less critical systems may only require periodic backups.

Organizations should also implement disaster recovery (DR) solutions that integrate with their backup systems, ensuring that data can be quickly restored in the event of a failure or disaster.

In large-scale environments, backup testing is critical for ensuring that the backup solution is working as expected and that data can be successfully recovered. As filesystems scale, the complexity of testing backups increases, as there may be more data to verify and more potential points of failure. Regular testing of backups ensures that organizations can meet their RTO and RPO objectives and that recovery processes are efficient and reliable. Testing should include both full system restores and file-level restores to ensure that the backup system can handle a wide range of recovery scenarios. Automated backup testing tools can help streamline this process by verifying the integrity of backup data and ensuring that it can be restored correctly.

Managing filesystem growth and scaling backup solutions is an ongoing process that requires careful planning and execution. As data volumes increase, the backup strategy must evolve to ensure that data is consistently protected without overburdening system resources or storage capacity. By leveraging technologies such as cloud storage, data deduplication, incremental backups, and centralized management solutions, organizations can build scalable and efficient backup systems that keep pace with their growing data needs. Regular testing, monitoring, and optimization of backup solutions are essential for ensuring that backup operations remain effective as filesystems continue to expand. With the right tools, processes, and strategies in place, organizations can successfully manage filesystem growth while maintaining a reliable and efficient backup solution.

Future Trends in Filesystem Management and Backup Strategies

As the volume of data continues to increase at an exponential rate, the strategies and technologies used for filesystem management and backup solutions must evolve to address new challenges and opportunities. The growing reliance on data-driven decisions, digital transformation, and cloud services is reshaping how organizations approach data storage, management, and protection. In the coming years, we can expect significant advances in filesystem management and backup strategies that will make them more efficient, secure, and scalable. Several trends are already emerging that will likely define the future of data management and backup, ranging from the rise of cloud-native technologies to the increasing importance of AI and machine learning in automating and optimizing backup processes.

One of the most notable trends in filesystem management is the shift toward distributed filesystems and cloud-native storage solutions. Traditional on-premises storage systems are becoming increasingly inadequate to handle the volume, velocity, and variety of data generated by modern applications. Distributed filesystems, such as Google File System (GFS), Hadoop Distributed File System (HDFS), and more recently, cloud-native filesystems like Amazon EFS and Microsoft Azure Files, are designed to scale horizontally, making them well-suited for environments that require high availability, durability, and fault tolerance. These systems allow organizations to store data across multiple nodes and regions, ensuring that data is protected even in the event of hardware failures or network disruptions. As businesses increasingly rely on cloud platforms for storage, the adoption of distributed filesystems will continue to grow, simplifying management and scaling storage resources on-demand.

Alongside the shift toward distributed filesystems, the future of backup strategies will be shaped by the increasing adoption of cloud storage solutions. Cloud-based backup solutions offer organizations the ability to store data offsite, providing an added layer of protection against local disasters, such as fires or theft, and reducing the risk of data loss. Cloud storage also offers unmatched scalability, allowing businesses to scale their backup storage seamlessly as their data grows. As cloud storage providers continue to innovate, backup strategies will increasingly integrate with cloud-native tools to automate and streamline backup processes. For example, cloud backup platforms may incorporate intelligent tiering, which automatically moves data to the most cost-effective storage tier based on usage patterns, further optimizing backup storage costs. The flexibility and accessibility of cloud backup solutions will continue to make them the preferred choice for many organizations, particularly those with large-scale or dynamic data storage requirements.

Another key trend in the future of filesystem management and backup strategies is the increasing use of artificial intelligence (AI) and machine learning (ML) to optimize backup operations. AI and ML algorithms are being integrated into backup software to enhance automation, improve data classification, and predict potential failures before they occur. By analyzing large volumes of backup data, these algorithms can identify patterns and anomalies, helping organizations proactively address potential issues. For instance, AI could be used to optimize backup schedules, ensuring that backups are performed during periods of low system load, or to predict when a disk or storage device is likely to fail, allowing for preemptive action to avoid data loss. Additionally, AI-powered systems could automatically prioritize critical data for backup, ensuring that mission-critical systems are always protected, while less important data can be backed up less frequently.

As organizations continue to embrace hybrid and multi-cloud environments, filesystem management and backup strategies will need to adapt to these complex infrastructures. Hybrid cloud solutions, which combine on-premises storage with public and private cloud resources, offer organizations the flexibility to store and manage data where it makes the most sense. Backup solutions in hybrid environments must be able to seamlessly integrate with various cloud platforms, ensuring that data is consistently protected regardless of where it resides. Multi-cloud strategies, where organizations use multiple cloud providers to avoid vendor lock-in and improve redundancy, will also require backup solutions that can operate across different cloud platforms with ease. Future backup strategies will increasingly be designed with flexibility and interoperability in mind, enabling organizations to manage backups across hybrid and multi-cloud environments without creating silos of data or complicating recovery processes.

Another area where future trends are likely to make a significant impact is in the realm of data privacy and security. With the increasing volume of sensitive and personal data being stored, organizations must ensure that their backup solutions adhere to stringent privacy and security standards. As regulatory requirements such as the General Data Protection Regulation (GDPR) and the California Consumer Privacy Act (CCPA) continue to evolve, filesystem management and backup strategies will need to incorporate advanced encryption and access control mechanisms to safeguard data. Future backup solutions will likely include end-to-end encryption by default, ensuring that data is protected both in transit and at rest. Additionally, zero-trust security models, which assume that no device or user can be trusted by default, will become more prevalent in backup solutions. This will involve implementing strong authentication, continuous monitoring, and granular access controls to ensure that only authorized personnel can access or modify backup data.

The integration of blockchain technology into backup solutions is also a trend worth monitoring. Blockchain, with its decentralized and immutable nature, has the potential to provide a new level of transparency and security to backup processes. By leveraging blockchain, organizations could create an immutable record of backup activities, ensuring that backup data cannot be tampered with or deleted without trace. This could be particularly beneficial for industries that require high levels of data integrity and auditability, such as finance, healthcare, and legal sectors. Blockchain-based backup systems could also simplify data recovery by providing a transparent and verifiable history of backup versions, making it easier to restore data to a specific point in time without concerns over data manipulation.

In parallel with these technological advancements, there is also a growing focus on reducing the environmental impact of data storage and backup. As data centers continue to grow in size and number, their energy consumption and carbon footprint have become a major concern. Future filesystem management and backup solutions will likely incorporate more energy-efficient storage technologies and processes to reduce their environmental impact. This may include the use of green data centers, more energy-efficient hardware, and algorithms that minimize the power required for backup operations. Additionally, organizations will continue to explore storage optimization techniques such as data deduplication and compression, which reduce the amount of data that needs to be stored, thereby lowering energy consumption.

The future of filesystem management and backup strategies will be heavily influenced by the ongoing growth of data, advancements in cloud technologies, and innovations in AI and security. As organizations face increasing pressure to manage larger datasets while ensuring data protection, backup solutions will become more automated, intelligent, and integrated into the broader IT ecosystem. Cloud-native solutions, AI-powered optimization, hybrid and multi-cloud integration, and enhanced security measures will all play key roles in shaping the next generation of filesystem management and backup strategies. The continuous evolution of these technologies will not only improve backup performance and efficiency but also ensure that data remains secure and accessible, even in the face of growing data challenges.